Things Most Surely Believed

EVIDENCE ESSAYS

Charles C. Pugh III

Foreword by Bert Thompson, Ph.D.

Library of Congress Cataloging-in-Publication Data
Pugh, III, Charles C.
Things most surely believed: evidence essays/Charles C. Pugh III
Library of Congress Control Number: 2002095322

ISBN: 0-9725498-0-3
1. Apologetics 2. Philosphy of religion 3. Theology–doctrinal 4. Title

Cover Design by
Jerry Harris, Shreveport, LA

Scripture references are taken from The New King James Version, copyright Thomas Nelson, Inc. Other versions used are American Standard Version (ASV), King James Version (KJV), New American Standard Version (NASV), and New International Version (NIV).

Printed in the United States of America by
Schlabach Printers, Ltd.
2881 State Route 93
Sugarcreek, Ohio 44681

To

Mendy

Chip

Nicole

CONTENTS

ACKNOWLEDGMENTS

Without the help of many others this work would not have made it to completion. Thanks to my wife, Sharon, for her encouragement to complete this project. Thanks to the elders, churches, and individual brethren who give moral, spiritual, and financial support to my writing. Thanks to Lyn Miller for typing, research and editing assistance, and tirelessly contributing her organizational and professional skills to help see this volume completed. Thanks to Jerry Harris for the cover design, and appreciation to Bert Thompson for writing the Foreword. Thanks to Terry Varner for his words of recommendation and encouragement. Thanks to all who proofread the book before printing. Above all, thanks to Him Who has "stood with me and strengthened me. . . To Him be glory forever and ever. Amen!" (2 Timothy 4:17-18).

FOREWORD

Unlike many religions, Christianity always has been based in historical fact. From the historicity of Jesus Himself, to the reality of His resurrection, Christianity has competed in the marketplace of ideas with factuality as its formidable foundation.

While it may be true to say that some religions flourish best in secrecy, such is not the case with Christianity. It is intended to be presented, and to be defended, in the swirling maelstrom that is the public eye. In addition, while some religions eschew open investigation and critical evaluation, Christianity welcomes both. And so it should, since of all the major religions based upon an individual rather than a mere ideology, Christianity is the only one that claims, and can document, an empty tomb for its Founder. As British author Graham Fisher observed:

> A faith which cannot withstand the searing heat of rational logic is not **true** faith at all, and, no matter how successfully one can build subsequent belief systems from is unqualified axioms, it will always be no more stable than a house of cards, ready to fall at the slightest wind or the mildest shaking of its foundations. . .
>
> The Christian faith is the one major belief-system which bares its soul to its inner-most depths and challenge skeptics to make a diagnosis. . .
>
> The rationale of Christianity is based solidly in an event, not an idea. An event can be put under the critical microscope of historical investigation and can be interpreted logically and rationally. It matters not a whit what we believe in our hearts, it is what our heads tell us, as a result of honest inquiry, which must count. But it matters a great deal how we react to the results of that investigation for if our investigation reveals that this dead man actually did rise from the dead

> then He was no ordinary man, nor were His teachings merely great human wisdom. His resurrection, if true, confirms the truth-claims made for Him as being true and makes His other words authoritative too (*Why Believe in Adam?*, 1990, pp. 13, 16, 17, emp. in orig.).

Christianity is the religion of **knowledge** and **surety**. This, in fact, was the very concept behind Luke's comment in chapter one, verse one of the gospel that bears his name when he wrote: "Forasmuch as many have taken in hand to set forth in order **a declaration of those things which are most surely believed among us**, even as they delivered them unto us, **who from the beginning were eyewitnesses...**"

Anyone who would suggest that Christianity is based on an unproven (and unprovable) belief system nebulously termed "faith," robs Christianity of one of its most important constructs-verifiability that is rooted in historical fact based on eyewitness testimony.

Knowledge and truth are precious commodities. As a body of factual information and legitimate principles, knowledge is indispensable in human relationships. Truth, as knowledge justifiably believed, represents a fundamental reality of life that transcends both the provincial and the temporal. In their book, *Unshakable Foundations*, Norman Geisler and Peter Bocchino noted:

> Truth by its very nature is: noncontradictory-it does not violate the basic laws of logic; absolute-it does not depend upon any time, places, or conditions; discovered-it exists independently of the mind, we do not create it; descriptive-it is the agreement of the mind with reality; inescapable-to deny its existence is to affirm it (we are bound by it); and unchanging-it is the firm standard by which truth claims are measured (2001, p. 52, parenthetical comment in orig.).

He who possesses correct knowledge has within himself the potential to discern, and then act upon, truth. Knowledge frees from the shackles of ignorance; truth frees from the shackles of error. Indeed, knowledge and truth **are** precious commodities.

While almost anyone you ask will admit, **in theory**, that knowledge and truth are indispensable attributes of a sensible, everyday existence, **in practice** many people live out that daily existence as if knowledge and truth ultimately do not matter. Much of mankind lives according to an abstract, confusing, and largely inconsistent system of personal behavior. This is a bit odd, to say the least. In most matters, a man likely will insist upon complete **objectivity**. For example, in regard to his eating habits he might say, "I will not eat this food; it contains bacterial toxins that will kill me." In regard to matters of civil law, he might suggest, "That action is illegal; it violates my rights."

Yet when it comes to religion in general, and Christianity in particular, **subjectivity** rules the day. People can be so certain about their beliefs in the physical realm, but so nebulous about their beliefs in the spiritual realm. For example, on occasion when a person who believes in God is asked if God does, in fact, exist, he may say, "I **believe** He exists," or "I **hope** He exists," or "I **think** He exists." But rarely to you hear him say boldly, "I **know** He exists." Or, if a Christian is asked the question, "Do you know you are saved?," the response may go something like this: "I **believe** that I am," or "I **hope** that I am," or "I **think** that I am." But rarely do you hear someone confidently assert, "Yes, I **know** that I am saved."

This is indeed a sad state of affairs. We now have progressed to the point where in matters as mundane as food choices or legal wrangling, objectivity is an absolute requirement. Meanwhile, in the much more important area of spiritual matters, we not only expect, but in many cases insist upon, a subjectivity that we would not tolerate in any other sphere of our lives. It is as if the pluralistic postmodernism that has affected secular society (the "I'm OK, you're OK" or "Who am I to judge?" concept) finally has made its way into the spiritual community as well. Apparently, some among us either once knew but long since have forgotten, or never really understood in the first place, the proper relationship between truth and faith. Similarly, we either have forgotten, or no longer care about, the damage that an improper concept of truth and its relationship to faith can cause.

The time has come for Christians to embolden themselves once again with the same high regard for truth and faith that Jesus expressed when He stated: "And ye shall **know** the truth, and the truth shall make you free" (John 8:32, emp. added). Christianity is not an "I-hope-so/pie-in-the-sky/by-and-by" kind of religion based upon some esoteric, fairy-tale-like concept known as "faith." Rather, it is rooted and grounded in the provable existence of the one true God and the verifiable nature of the historical facts surrounding the life, death, and resurrection of His Son. When the apostle John wrote to comfort and reassure first-century Christians who found themselves in the midst of numerous trials and persecutions, he said: "These things have I written unto you, that ye may **know** that ye have eternal life, even unto you that believe on the name of the Son of God" (1 John 5:13, emp. added). Thus, according to both Jesus and John, a person not only can know something, but he can know that he knows it.

There are certain undeniable, critically important implications standing behind this kind of firm, confident declaration. Consider the following. If a person cannot **know** (with certainty) that God exists, then he cannot know (with certainty) that the Bible is His inspired Word. If a person cannot know that the Bible is the inspired Word of God, then he cannot know that Jesus is God's Son, since the Bible provides the evidentiary basis for such a claim. If a person cannot know that Christ is God's Son, then he cannot know that he is saved. Yet John specifically stated: "These things have I written unto you, that ye may **know** that ye have eternal life."

Christians are not agnostics! The agnostic suggests, "I **cannot know** whether God exists." Christians, on the other hand, **know** that God exists (see Psalm 46:10). Consider the alternative. Do Christians serve a God Who "may" or "may not" exist? Do Christians believe, and ask others to believe, the testimony of a Bible that "may" or "may not" be inspired? Do Christians place their faith in, trust, and obey a Christ Who "may" or "may not" be the Son of God? Hardly!

Even the casual reader will discern the close relationship among these vital issues. Knowledge of God's existence is foundational to faith (Psalm 46:10; Hebrews 11:6). Faith in Christ's

Sonship is pivotal to a person's salvation (John 8:24). An understanding of the nature of the verbal, plenary inspiration of the Bible is critical to an individual's daily walk with God (2 Timothy 3:16-17).

We live in a society in which an examination of the evidence behind a claim has become practically an everyday occurrence. Whether we are purchasing an automobile or considering an advertiser's boasts about its products, we routinely investigate a veritable plethora of evidences that can prove, or disprove, what is being said. The Bible teaches that mankind is lost and in desperate need of salvation-salvation that comes only through Jesus Christ. More often than not, the person who accepts and obeys the biblical message undergoes a radical change in both his thinking and his lifestyle. Surely the grand nature of Christianity's claim is such that it invites and requires both investigation and verification. For someone to suggest that Christianity, or the life-altering changes it ushers in, is based on little more than an unproven assertion (which, in the end, might or might not be true) hardly could be viewed as a rational approach that would commend itself to intelligent people.

Surely, people in the world who are not yet Christians, yet whom we hope to see become Christians, are smart enough to see through a ruse that asks them to "act as if" they know God exists, to "act as if" they know Jesus is His Son, or to "act as if" the Bible is His inspired Word when, in fact, they do not know any of those things at all. Further, if Christians simply "act like" they know, when in reality they do not, why are they not hypocrites? Furthermore, if the "as if" hypothesis of faith were correct, how would the Christian-who eventually will be forced to admit that he **does not really know** these things-be any different from the agnostic (who readily admits that he **cannot know** these things)?

If knowledge relates to the truth (John 8:32), then faith relates no less to Him Who is the truth (John 14:1, 6). Both faith (John 16:27-30) and knowledge (John 7:17) realize that He and His teaching are from the Father. The apostle Peter's desire was that Christians "grow in the grace and **knowledge** of our Lord Jesus Christ" (2 Peter 3:18). Peter's fellow apostle, Paul, expressed "the desire that ye might be filled with the **knowledge** of his will in all wisdom and spiritual understanding" (Colossians 1:9). God's desire is that "all men be saved and come unto the **knowledge** of the truth" (1 Timothy 2:4). Paul's statement, "I **know** him whom I have believed. . ." (2 Timothy 1:12) is beyond all comprehension unless one understands the correct relationship between faith and knowledge. Furthermore, not only can men **know** the truth, but they also can **know** that they know it, as the apostle John emphasized repeatedly. John stated that we can **know** the truth (1 John 2:21). Similarly, he noted that we can "know that we know" Jesus and "**know** that we are in him" as we keep His commandments or His word (1 John 2:3,5). Also, we can "**know** that we are of the truth" (1 John 3:14, 19). Thus, John summed up this sentiment by saying simply, "We **know** that we are of God" (1 John 5:19; cf. John 7:16-17).

Isaiah used the terms "know" and "believe" synonymously with reference to God Himself: "Ye are my witnesses, saith Jehovah, and my servant whom I have chosen; that ye may **know** and **believe** me, and understand that I am he: before me there was no God formed, neither shall there be after me. I , even I, am Jehovah; and besides me there is no savior" (Isaiah 43:10-11). On one occasion, when Jesus was having a conversation with the Jews about His status as the Son of God, He said to them: "Except ye **believe** that I am he, ye shall die in your sins" (John 8:24). Yet in that same context, He stated that eventually those same Jews could "**know** that I am he, and that I do nothing of myself, but as the Father taught me" (8:28). The Lord also used faith and knowledge synonymously in John 17:21-23:

> That they may all be one; even as thou, Father, are in me, and I in thee, that they also may be in us: that the world may **believe** that thou didst send me. And the glory which thou has given me I have given unto them; that they may be one, even as we are one; I in them, and thou in me, that they may be perfected into one; that the world may **know** that thou didst send me, and lovedst them, even as thou lovedst me.

He further advised the Jews: "If I do not the works of my Father, believe me not. But if I do, though ye believe not me, believe the works: that ye may **know**, and **believe**, that the Father is in me, and I in him" (John 10:37-38). From Christ's vantage point, there was no distinction between faith and knowledge. Clearly, faith and knowledge are neither mutually exclusive nor diametrically opposed. These scriptures teach that for faith to be rock-solid, truly biblical faith, it must be founded on fact.

It is that type of faith-built upon facts "most surely believed among us"-that Charles C. Pugh III addresses in this book. He begins with Luke's preface to his gospel, and proceeds from there to document the foundational evidence upon which New Testament Christianity is constructed. Via his discussions about the nature of faith and evidence, and how logic and human reason fit into the process of building a rock-solid faith, Charles not only establishes the truthfulness of the Christian religion, but also "the greatness of Christianity" (which, not coincidentally happens to be the title of the last chapter of his book).

I have known Charles Pugh III for more than two decades. He is a good friend, a respected preacher, and an extremely capable teacher. His pen is powerful-but no more so than the Gospel message it proclaims and defends. Read *Things Most Surely Believed* with an open mind and a searching heart, and it will open to you vistas of which you may only have dreamed. If you are already a Christian, it will make you justifiably proud to be an "heir of God, and joint-heir with Christ" (Romans 8:17). If you are not a Christian, this book will show you not only **why** you should become one, but **how** to do so. I bid you good reading. You are in for a fascinating and instructive literary journey.

Bert Thompson, Ph.D.
Former professor, College of Veterinary Medicine, Texas A&M University
Currently, Executive Director, Apologetics Press, Montgomery, Alabama

INTRODUCTION

The field of study, which relates to the refutation of unbelief, and the defense of Christianity, is called ***Christian Apologetics***. It is also called ***Christian Evidences***, because it involves the study of the evidence upon which the case for Christianity exists. Christian Apologetics (Evidences) deals with the evidence for (1) the existence of God (2) the inspiration of the Bible and (3) the deity of Jesus of Nazareth. This involves both an offensive and a defensive strategy. The offensive strategy entails a strong, militant (yet kind and loving) proclamation of the gospel of Christ (Matt. 28:18-20; Mark 16:15-16; Luke 24:46-47). The defensive strategy entails a refutation of every attack on the truth of the gospel of Christ (Philip. 1:16; Titus 1:9; 1 Pet. 3:15; Jude 3).

For several years now there has been a shift from theism, and a move toward philosophies which not only deny God, but also deny such crucial matters as the rationality of man, the existence of truth, and the existence of an objective standard of morality.

It likely is the case that there are not many (if any) major college or university campuses in the United States where atheism or agnosticism are not defended in the classroom as viable approaches to human life. The theory of evolution is taught on university campuses as well as in elementary schools, not as mere theory which cannot be proved, but as established fact. Additionally, Christendom has been influenced by subjectivism which implies that contradictory doctrines may be believed and practiced, and *all* parties which adhere to such can be right while believing and practicing thusly. The church of Christ has been influenced by a "new hermeneutic" that denies the proper role of sound reasoning (logic) in the Christian life.

There is nothing more basic to a study of the Bible and the application of true Christianity than a study of Christian Apologetics or the evidence upon which the case for Christianity rests. That such is the case is seen in the fact that these matters deal with the very foundation of the ability of the human mind to reason correctly as it gathers evidence and draws conclusions in harmony with the evidence. If it is the case that (1) man cannot, and/or must not, use logic (sound reasoning) in religious and moral matters, (2) God does not exist, (3) the Bible is not the word of God, and (4) Jesus Christ is not the Son of God, then there is no valid reason why one ought to study the original languages of the Bible, attempt to ascertain the meaning of the biblical text (hermeneutics), or do anything else related to a study of the Bible. How could there be anything more basic than the study of Christian Evidences and various related areas (i.e. the Philosophy of Religion)?

This book has been published with the conviction that the issues with which it is concerned are some of the most basic and crucial in life. Although some of these issues deal with matters, which can, at times, be very complex, I have tried to write in such a way that both the certainty, and the practicality, of the message are clear. The pathway to Christian faith is not always easy, but the case is such that an honest person can become convinced of the truth of the things most surely believed and, in believing, ". . .rejoice with joy inexpressible and full of glory, receiving the end of your faith—the salvation of your souls" (1 Pet. 1:8-9). It is my fervent prayer that this volume will be used to this end.

–The Author

CHAPTER 1

LUKE'S PREFACE AND THE CASE FOR CHRISTIANITY

> Inasmuch as many have taken in hand to set in order a narrative of those things which are most surely believed among us, just as those who from the beginning were eyewitnesses and ministers of the word delivered them to us, it seemed good to me also, having had perfect understanding of all things from the very first, to write to you an orderly account, most excellent Theophilus, that you may know the certainty of those things in which you were instructed (Luke 1:1-4).

The above four verses form one single sentence in the original Greek. It is one of the most remarkable sentences in the New Testament. Its implications are profound with respect to the apologetic value possessed therein. Robertson observed, "It ranks with the introductions of Herodotus and Thucydides for brevity, modesty and dignity. It is couched in purest literary Koine" (18). Hendriksen compares this preface/prologue of Luke's gospel to those of such Greek medical men as Hippocrates, Dioscorides, and Galen; the historians Herodotus, Thucydides, and Polybius; and the biographer Plutarch. However he stated, "His prologue is more beautifully balanced than any of the others and also kinder in tone than some of them" (Hendriksen 54). We believe it surpasses all and bears marks which attest to the claim that Christianity is the one true religion.

Exposition

VERSE ONE: ***"Inasmuch. . ."Forasmuch"*** (KJV). The conjunction in Greek is ***epeideiper*** from ***epei*** (since), ***dei*** (it is so), and ***per*** (it could not be otherwise, Godet 34). It points to something that is a well-known fact for justifying an action that has been (or will be) taken.

" . . . as many have taken in hand. . ." Many is from ***polloi*** (the most, the majority, great multitude, Brown 95). Cf. Matt. 7:13, 22; Luke 1:14. ***Taken in hand*** means "to put one's hand to, undertake, seek, attempt" (Hendriksen 61).

" . . . to set in order. . ." From ***anatassomai*** (to put together in order, arrange, compose, Thayer 47).

" . . . a narrative. . ." (diegesis). The King James Version renders it "a declaration." It refers to an "account" (Arndt and Gingrich 194). It involves fullness of detail (Moulton and Milligan 161).

" . . . of those things . . ." This is not a question of mere narratives, but of actual historical facts, things that have really taken place (Geldenhuys 56).

" . . . most surely believed among us, . . ." The American Standard Version has "have been fulfilled." Here the events are thought of as completed. The perfect passive participle is used here to indicate the permanent state after the completed action (Geldenhuys 56). In connection with persons it may mean surely believed (Rom. 4:21) and means to cause conviction which leaves no room for doubt (Godet 35). When it refers to a fact it signifies complete accomplishment (35); events that accomplished a preconceived plan (36). Cf. John 20:30 and John 1:14.

VERSE TWO: ***"just as. . .***; "even as" (***kathos***). Meaning "indicating comparison" (Arndt and Gingrich 392); "in conformity with that which" (Godet 36). Cf. Matt. 21:6; 28:6; Luke 11:1; John. 1:23; Acts 15:8.

". . . those who from the beginning. . ." Lamar says, "The word is restricted by the term eyewitnesses to the ***public*** beginning i.e. the entrance of Christ upon his ministry; or, as more definitely explained by Luke himself, the time of his baptism (Acts 1:22)" (17-18). Cf. John 15:27.

" . . . were eyewitnesses and ministers of the word. . ." Hendriksen states, "Note that Luke does not include himself among the eyewitnesses but among those to whom those eyewitnesses handed down their reports and testimonies. That the term ***eyewitness*** includes earwitness is clear from 1 John 1:1" (56). Luke lays special emphasis on the fact that this material is that which has really happened and has been communicated by authoritative witnesses. He claims to be dealing, not with fabricated fables, but with actual events (cf. 2 Pet. 1:16ff).

". . . delivered them to us," From ***paradidomi*** which means "transmit, relate, teach" (Arndt and Gingrich 620). Cf. 1 Cor. 11:23; 15:3. "To hand down, pass on" (Brown 772).

VERSE THREE: ***"it seemed good to me also, . . ." Seemed*** is from ***dokeo***. Here Luke places himself on the same line with those mentioned in verse one who had set forth the evidence with regard to the case for Christianity. There is, however, another interesting connection between Luke's statement here and what he wrote in Acts 15:22, 25, 28. The word used is identical in all of these references including Luke 1:3. Acts 15:28 adds the thought "to the Holy Spirit" to the phrase "it then pleased the apostles and elders, with the whole church" (v. 22) and "it seemed good to us" (v. 25). These statements provide a connective basis between (1) the divine purpose entailed in inspiration and (2) the use of human instrumentality to accomplish that purpose. "This does not affirm some type of mechanical dictation view of inspiration as the Bible writers were not totally passive in this process of inspiration" (Laws 25). As to the details of how this was accomplished, the Bible does not make such known. However, it does make it clear that in some fashion ***no*** prophecy (i.e. prophetic writing, scripture) ever "came by the will of man, but holy men of God spoke as they were moved by the Holy Spirit" (2 Pet. 1:20-21). Some excellent observations on these matters are found in Deaver (320-328).

" . . . having had perfect understanding of all things. . ."
" . . . having traced the course of all things accurately" (ASV).
" . . . carefully investigated everything from the beginning" (NIV).

Lamar says:

> "The Greek . . . indicates a process rather than . . . a result. The meaning is, that he had ***carefully investigated*** the things which he was about to write, and by ***diligent research*** had become ***accurately informed*** upon them. . . . This employment of natural faculties and ordinary means is in harmony with the highest and best conceptions of inspiration . . . " (18).

Robertson explains:

> "Luke means that he had instituted a process of research in his inquiries concerning the life of Christ that covered 'all things.' It was, therefore, a thorough and careful investigation that began at the beginning, from the first, meaning with the birth of John the Baptist, as the sequel shows" (51).

He did this "accurately, exactly" (Thayer 51). He not only made an investigation, but he did it perfectly and accurately.

" . . . from the very first, . . ." First or ***beginning*** is from Gk. ***anothen***. Cf. John 3:3,7; 19:11. In Mark 15:38 it is rendered ***top*** (i.e. the veil of the temple was torn from top to bottom). "Both in and outside the NT a. an adv. of place 'from above' (Mt. 27:51) . . . b. adv. of time 'from an earlier period' (Acts 26:5) . . . c. 'From the first' (Luke. 1:3) d. 'anew' (Gal. 4:9)" (Buchsel 378). Gaussen, as cited by Lamar, renders ***anothen*** in Luke 1:3 "from above" as in John 3:31 and understands it as Luke's claim of inspiration (18).

" . . . to write to you . . ." Write is from the verb ***grapho***. "Certain writers made reference to their own writing . . . to guarantee the truth of the message (Luke. 1:3 f.; Philip. 3:11; 1 John 2:21; 5:13; Rev. 19:9)" (Brown 489). The noun ***graphe*** is used 51 times in the N. T. and "in the NT is used exclusively of Holy Scripture" (490).

" . . . an orderly account. . ." It means "in order, one after the other of sequence in time, space, or logic" (Arndt and Gingrich 389). It does not necessarily point to chronological order but also

logical considerations. "Luke's word occurs in Acts 11:4 concerning Peter's discourse in Jerusalem about the events in Caesarea which Blass interprets to be a full recital without important omissions, a complete series rather than a chronological sequence" (Robertson 53). Ramsay, as cited by Robertson, takes it to be "a rational order" (14).

". . . *most excellent Theophilus, . . .*" Theophilus means "lover of God" or "dear to God." Who was this one to whom both Luke's gospel account and the Acts of the Apostles are addressed (cf. Luke 1:3; Acts 1:1)? The title by which he is addressed - "most excellent" - is one of rank applied by Luke to both Felix and Festus (Acts 22:26; 24:3; 26:25). Thus, "it is likely that he was a chief magistrate in some city of Greece or Asia Minor. In all probability, he was a Gentile convert" (Cox 3).

VERSE FOUR: ***"that you may know. . ." Know*** is from ***epiginosko***: "know exactly, completely, through and through" (Arndt and Gingrich 290); "know accurately, know well" (Thayer 237).

" . . . the certainty of those things. . ." Certainty here is ***asphaleia***. It was used to refer to proofs, written security, security in a commercial sense, contracts and title-deeds (Moulton and Milligan 88). In Acts 5:23 it is used to refer to the prison doors which were shut ***securely***. The word was a technical law term and was used to refer to the convincing nature of an argument. ***Asphalos*** is used in Acts 2:36; 16:23. This is a powerful term and refers to the "irrefragable certainty of the facts of the gospel" (Godet 39).

" . . . in which you were instructed." Instructed is from ***katecheo*** which means teach, instruct. Cf. Acts 18:25; Rom. 2:18; Gal. 6:6. Although Theophilus had been taught, he would be edified and strengthened, as he was furnished with Luke's orderly and logical presentation of facts and evidences. Cf. 1 John 5:13. Luke desired Theophilus to truly understand that the faith which he had been taught had an impregnable historical foundation.

Implications

This preface sentence of Luke contains profound implications that attest to the truthfulness of the case for Christianity. These implications press on every honest thinking person the clear claims of the New Testament writers. These implications cannot be dismissed with a wave of the hand or some cute quibble. The fact is, they cannot rationally be dismissed at all. They serve, with the totality of available evidence, as proof that the religion of Jesus Christ is true. Some, but not all, of the implications in Luke's prologue, relative to the nature of the case for Christianity, are that the religion of Jesus Christ is one of (1) ***Publicity*** (2) ***Credibility*** (3) ***Authenticity*** and (4) ***Certainty***.

Publicity. Luke begins with the claim that the Christian religion rests not upon events which affected merely a private few, but ***many***. In one of his masterful defenses of the faith, the apostle Paul appealed to King Agrippa's knowledge of this matter when he said, "The king before whom I also speak freely, knows these things; for I am convinced that none of these things escapes his attention, since this thing was not done in a corner" (Acts 26:26). Peter used this same evidence of publicity when he told the multitudes on Pentecost that Jesus of Nazareth was a Man attested by God through the evidence of miracles, wonders, and signs "in your midst, as you yourselves also know" (Acts 2:22). The record of the statement of some of the earliest enemies of Christianity admits this. They said, "That a notable miracle has been done . . . is evident to all who dwell in Jerusalem, and we cannot deny it" (Acts 4:16). NO OTHER RELIGION HAS THIS EVIDENCE OF HISTORICAL PUBLICITY AS DOES CHRISTIANITY.

Credibility. On what basis could one ***rationally*** dismiss Luke's statements as not credible?

> Either an author who begins with a declaration such as that (in his preface) had mixed freely with many of the eyewitnesses . . . in the events which he proceeds to record, or he is a thorough impostor, who consciously and deliberately aims at producing belief in his exceptional qualifications in order to gain credit for his History. If the author was an impostor, his work remains one of the most incomprehensible and unintelligible facts in literary history (Robertson 55-56).

Authenticity. Luke, with the skilled precision of the physician he was, claimed an accurate dissection of the data before him. This is not the evidence of a slipshod writer, but of one who claims to have carefully investigated and drawn only such conclusions as could be warranted by the evidence. He claims his presentation is a rational and logical one.

Certainty. Nothing in this statement of Luke is any clearer than his claim that the propositions of Christianity are ***certain*** and ***secure***. As Geldenhuys has stated:

> It is a historic fact that when Luke wrote his Gospel there existed among many educated persons of the time a strong desire for firmly established truth in religion. The various philosophic systems left them unsatisfied, the popular pagan religions filled them with repugnance and they yearned for trustworthy knowledge concerning religious matters. To such a seeker after well-established truth Luke addresses himself, and through him to all other persons who feel the need of knowing the glad tidings with full certainty. It is Luke's earnest desire that as regards their knowledge of the Gospel they shall have firm ground beneath their feet (54).

Conclusion

Words fail to adequately describe the greatness of this sentence written by the beloved physician (Col. 4:14) 2000 years ago. It, as well as other statements written by this devoted researcher of sacred history, have been viciously attacked by the various critics. However, the statement, with its clear claims and rational appeal, has outlived (and will outlive) all the critics. The reason? Its ultimate greatness and endurance is realized in the fact that it is Scripture (cf. 1 Tim. 5:18; Luke 10:7).

More than one hundred years ago, Lawrence W. Scott wrote a work entitled, *Hand-Book of Christian Evidence Or Facts Against Infidelity*. In it he wrote what is a wonderful summation of the basic claims and implications of Luke 1:1-4. He stated:

> . . . *Christianity is a religion of fact; that it rests upon incontrovertible facts–facts attested by the very best and most reliable historic testimony in existence.* Our religious teachers should show a bold front, and evince that they are ready to defend the truth "against all comers and goers."

> They should plant themselves squarely upon the Rock of Ages, and defiantly exclaim, in the language of James Fitz-James: — "Come one, come all! This rock shall fly from its firm base as soon as I!" (xvi).

The case for Christianity will *never* fly from its firm base! And may we ever be anchored to it!

WORKS CITED

Arndt, William F. and Wilbur F. Gingrich. *A Greek-English Lexicon of the New Testament and Other Early Christian Literature.* 1957. Chicago: U of Chicago P, 1973.

Brown, Colin, ed. *The New International Dictionary of New Testament Theology*. Vol. 3:Pri-Z. Grand Rapids: Zondervan, 1978. 3 vols.

Buchsel, Friedrich. *Theological Dictionary of the New Testament.* 1964. Vol. 1 Grand Rapids: Wm. B. Eerdmans, 1977. 10 vols.

Cox, Frank L. *According To Luke*. Austin: Firm Foundation, 1941.

Deaver, Roy. "What The Bible Means By Inspiration And Revelation - Defining and Clarifying" *21st Annual Spiritual Sword Lectureship*. Pulaski: Sain Publications, 1996.

Geldenhuys, Norval. *Commentary on the Gospel of Luke*. Grand Rapids: Wm. B. Eerdmans, 1977.

Godet, F. *A Commentary on the Gospel of St. Luke*. New York: I.K. Funk & Co., 1881.

Hendricksen, William. *New Testament Commentary*. Grand Rapids: Baker, 1978.

Lamar, J. S. *The New Testament Commentary-Luke*. St. Louis: Christian Board of Publication, 1877.

Laws, Jim. "The Argument for The Inspiration of The Bible". *21st Annual Spiritual Sword Lectureship.* Pulaski: Sain Publications, 1996.

Moulton, James Hope and Milligan, George. *The Vocabulary of the Greek New Testament.* 1930. Grand Rapids: Wm. B. Eerdmans, 1976.

Robertson, A. T. *Luke The Historian in the Light of Research.* Edinburgh: T&T Clark, 1920.

Scott, Laurence W. *Hand-Book of Christian Evidence or Facts Against Infidelity.* 1880. Cincinnati: F. L. Rowe, 1914.

Thayer, Joseph Henry. *Greek-English Lexicon of The New Testament.* 1962. Grand Rapids: Zondervan, 1973.

CHAPTER 2

FAITH AND EVIDENCE

"Now faith is the substance of things hoped for, the evidence of things not seen" (Heb. 11:1). This is the only verse in the Bible in which the words ***faith*** and ***evidence*** appear together. However, as we will observe in this chapter, there is a sense in which evidence is implied every time the Scriptures refer to acceptable faith.

Faith is the ***substance*** (***assurance***, ASV) of things hoped for. ***Substance*** is from the Greek, ***hupostasis***. It means:

> The whole body of documents bearing on the ownership of a person's property, deposited in the archives, and forming the evidence of ownership... In all cases there is the same central idea of something that underlies visible conditions and guarantees a future possession... Faith is the title - deed of things hoped for (Moulton and Milligan 660).

Faith is the ***evidence*** (***conviction***, ASV) of things not seen. The word ***evidence***, is from ***elenchos*** and was used to refer to the proof, or evidence, used to substantiate a law-suit in a court (202). It means "a proof; that by which a thing is proved or tested" (Thayer 202). The verb, ***elencho***, means "to give evidence in 'the' matter... supply the proofs... make an inquiry and state the facts" (Moulton and Milligan 202). It should be obvious to everyone who studies these matters that it is the case that there is a conjunction between biblical faith and evidence. In this chapter we will consider three areas which can help us in understanding this relationship between faith and evidence. These areas are (1) a ***law*** which implies the conjunction of faith and evidence, (2) a ***leap*** which denies the conjunction of faith and evidence, and (3) a ***lesson*** which applies the conjunction of faith and evidence.

A Law

The law of rationality says that one should draw only such conclusions as are warranted by the evidence. Another way of saying this is that we ought to justify our conclusions by adequate evidence. The truth of the law of rationality is seen in the fact that the moment one asks, "How can I be sure it is true?" he proves its truth. He simply is asking for the sufficient evidence which proves the law is true. To put it another way, one who inquires as to the truth of the law of rationality is seeking the adequate evidence which proves it is the case that one ought to justify his conclusions by adequate evidence! Thus, the law of rationality is seen to be true on the very face of it. One could not even attempt to disprove it (i.e. setting forth evidence to negate it) without proving it.

Thompson has stated, "By ***evidence*** we mean what the term literally suggests, that which 'shows' or 'exhibits' or 'brings into view'. The evidence shows or brings into view the basis upon which the claim of truth rests" (44). In a logical context, evidence consists of statements called ***premises*** which imply the statement (proposition) which is believed to be true. For example, if X implies Y, then we can believe Y is true because of the evidence of X.

To be rational simply means that one honors the law rationality (i.e. he draws only such conclusions as are warranted by the evidence). The Bible teaches (1) the law of rationality is true and (2) all men ought to honor this law. Isaiah wrote, " 'Present your case', says the Lord, 'Bring forth your strong reasons, says the King of Jacob'" (Isa. 41:21). Paul wrote, "Prove all things..." (1 Thess. 5:21, ASV). John stated, "Beloved, believe not every spirit, but prove the spirits, whether they are of God; because many false prophets are gone out into the world" (1 John 4:1, ASV).

A Leap

Although it is the case that the Bible teaches Christian faith is rational, and God does not ask us to believe anything for which He does not give us sufficient evidence, some affirm that faith is irrational. They hold that Christian faith must involve the espousal of some inadequately supported conclusion by a "leap into the dark" beyond the available and relevant evidence. The following diagram contrasts the true view of Christian faith as set forth in the Sacred Scriptures with the false view that claims faith is some "leap into the dark" (Warren 15).

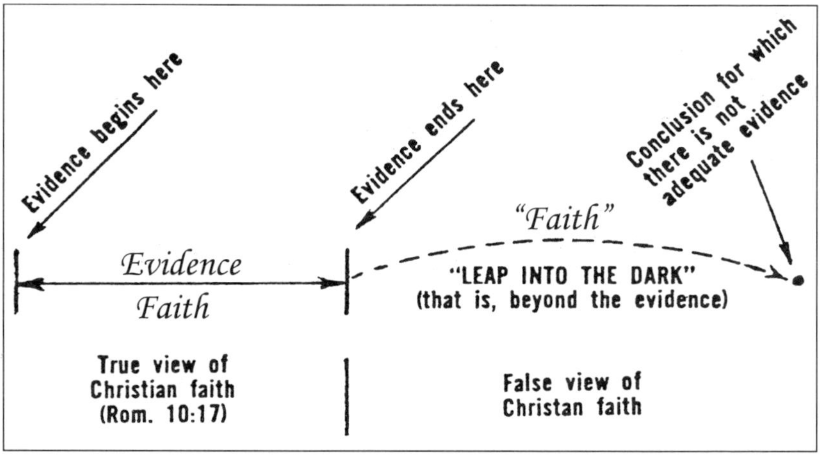

The Bible teaches that faith comes from the sufficient evidence provided by the Word of God (Rom. 10:17). To claim that faith is a "leap into the dark" beyond the evidence is to espouse irrationalism, which implies agnosticism, which implies that, for all we know, the Christian faith may not be true. This is not to say that one **fully** comprehends **all** the details of the basic propositions of the Christian faith (i.e. God exists, the Bible is the word of God, Jesus Christ is the Son of God, and to be saved one must believe in, love, and obey Jesus Christ). However, it is to say that God has provided sufficient revelation (evidence) for believing and knowing that Christianity is the one, true religion. There are sufficient reasons for being a Christian (cf. 1 Pet. 3:15). As Sweet has stated:

> The logical result of discrediting or depreciating human reason is agnosticism, which is a state of mind wherein the power of evidence is lost because of a fixed belief in the infirmity of the human mind as the organ of divine knowledge. The false and artificial antithesis which has often been established between reason and revelation spells ruin to the task of the apologist. Reason becomes a blind faculty which tells us nothing about God. Revelation becomes a sphere of extra-rational beliefs indistinguishable from superstition. Faith becomes an asylum for the feeble-minded. Christianity becomes a mode of interpreting the unknown, the truth of which it is impossible to establish on any recognizable rational grounds (16).

Where there is no revelation (evidence) from God there can be no true faith in God. No "Word of God" equals no "faith in God" (Rom. 10:17). God has spoken through two basic sources (volumes) of revelation: (1) General revelation and (2) Special revelation. General revelation includes the evidence He has set forth in (1) the world and (2) man. Special revelation includes the evidence set forth in (1) the Bible and (2) the Person and Work of Jesus Christ. The Bible implies the value, and adequacy, of general revelation to provide sufficient evidence to produce faith in the existence of God (Psalm 19:1-6; Acts 14:17; Rom. 1:20; Heb. 3:4, et al). The Bible also implies the necessity, and adequacy, of the special revelation that is set forth in the Sacred Scriptures as sufficient evidence to produce faith in, and obedience to, Jesus Christ (2 Tim. 3:14-17; 1 Cor. 2:7-14; John 20:30-31; 2 Pet. 1:16-21, et al). Christian faith is not a "leap into the dark", but a "walk in the light" provided by the sufficient evidence of God's revelation (1 John 1:1-7).

A Lesson

A lesson in John 20:24-31 applies the conjunction of faith and evidence. Thomas was not with the other apostles when Jesus made His first appearance to them (John 20:24). The others reported to Thomas that they had seen the Lord, but Thomas said, "Unless I see in His hands the prints of the nails, and put my finger into the print of the nails, and put my hand into His side, I will not believe" (John 20:25). In one sense, we respect and admire the attitude of Thomas. He implied an attitude which said, "Without evidence I will not believe. Give me the evidence, and I will believe." The Lord came and said to Thomas, "Reach your finger here, and look at My hands; and reach your hand here, and put it into My side. Do not be unbelieving, but believing" (John 20:27). The Lord gave Thomas the evidence. Then Thomas answered and said to Him, "My Lord and My God!" (John 20:28). When Thomas saw the evidence, he drew the conclusion warranted by the evidence.

Faith does not always mean the absence of sight. Sometimes faith and sight are contrasted (2 Cor. 5:7). However, the incident with regard to Thomas implies there can be faith where there is sight. The Lord said to Thomas, "Because you have seen Me, you have believed..." (John 20:29a). What Thomas saw, empirically, did not preclude his believing on Jesus. However, there can also be faith where there is no sight. Jesus also said to Thomas, "...Blessed are those who have not seen and yet have believed" (John 20:29b). [NOTE: The Lord rebuked all of the apostles for their failure to initially accept the valid testimony of "those who had seen Him after He had risen" (Mark 16:14)].

How do those who have not seen come to faith? Jesus said those who have not seen are blessed, because they draw the conclusion warranted by the evidence. It is not that they are blessed because they believe without evidence, but because they believe without sight. Following this statement of our Lord with regard to not seeing and yet believing, John wrote, "And truly Jesus did many other signs in the presence of His disciples, which are not written in this book; but these are written that you may believe that Jesus is the Christ, the Son of God, and that believing you may have life in His name" (John 20:30-31). The very existence of the written revelation presupposes the need for evidence to produce faith.

Conclusion

There is an essential conjunction between biblically approved faith and evidence. The law of rationality implies this conjunction of faith and evidence. Faith is not a "leap into the dark" beyond adequate evidence. The lesson learned from Thomas, as he desired to see the resurrected Lord before he believed, is that faith and evidence are essentially conjoined.

> We must remind ourselves that Christianity claims to be a rational system. It makes much of belief, and emphasizes strongly the necessity of faith as an organ of spiritual vision. As we have seen, however, faith (that is, trust beyond the range of experiment) is an element in all reasoning processes. Christianity admits the unprecedented nature of the events which it alleges in the career of Christ, but maintains that the belief in these events is entirely reasonable because they are supported by many infallible proofs (Sweet 92).

Works Cited

Moulton, James Hope and Milligan, George. *The Vocabulary of the Greek New Testament*. 1930. Grand Rapids: Wm. B. Eerdmans, 1976.

Sweet, Louis Matthew. *The Verification of Christianity*. Boston: The Gorham Press, 1920.

Thayer, Joseph Henry. *Greek-English Lexicon of The New Testament*. 1962. Grand Rapids: Zondervan, 1973.

Thompson, Samuel M. *A Modern Philosophy of Religion*. Chicago: Henry Regnery Company, 1955.

Warren, Thomas B. *Logic And The Bible*. Jonesboro: National Christian Press, 1982.

CHAPTER 3

LOGIC, REASON, AND THE BIBLE

Shirley MacLaine, pop theologian of the New Age movement, has written, "Don't evaluate and don't let your left brain judge what you are thinking. Give your left brain more space. As a matter of fact, don't think" (Geisler and Brooks 7). It would be difficult to imagine worse advice to give someone than to tell them not to think. Yet this kind of *misology* (the hatred or rejection of logic) and/or *logophobia* (the fear of logic) represents the extreme to which some in our society have gone in their thinking. Such twenty-first century non-thinking is counterpart to those whom Paul described as ". . . vain in their reasonings, and their senseless heart was darkened. Professing themselves to be wise, they became fools" (Rom. 1:21-22, ASV).

Although perhaps not to the extreme of MacLaine, or other New Age thinkers, there is a kind of misology and logophobia that is being manifested on the part of some among churches of Christ today who are calling for a "new hermeneutic". They claim that our old hermeneutic needs rejected because, among other reasons, it is a "thorough-going inductivism" (i.e. thorough detailed and slavish attention to inductive reasoning . . . Collier 4). This form of misology and/or logophobia opposes the view that the Bible is a "logical sourcebook" (Downs 7) and rejects "an inductive method of reasoning which views the Bible as a sourcebook of scientific, empirical, and factual data, which can be searched out by means of reason and formed into a logical system" (5). (One might ask in response: Does this mean that the Bible should be viewed as a source book of *unscientific, unverifiable, unfactual* data which cannot be searched out by means of sound reasoning but rather is built on an illogical [i.e., irrational] system?)

Logic — The *Essence* Of It

What is logic? Is it just a bunch of incomprehensible symbols and arbitrary rules that may be okay for professors in ivory towers but an unknown language to the man on the street? Isn't life deeper than logic? "Life is green, but logic is gray and lifeless", some say. Just mention the word–*LOGIC*–and you will see panic on the faces of some.

Simply stated, *logic* is the process of correct reasoning. Logic is not psychology. It is not mere wishing, or arguing in the sense of wrangling. It does not describe what people think about, or how they reach conclusions, but it describes how they *ought* to think in order to reason correctly. Logic has to do with *inference*. Logic is correctly inferring (deducing) what is implied by explicit statements (evidence). It is the study of *right* reason or correct inferences. It is the way to think so that we draw correct conclusions by understanding implications and the mistakes made in thinking. It is sound reasoning.

Logic — The *Effect* Of It

Logic is the most basic tool of any interpreter. Geisler and Brooks correctly affirm:

> Simply put, you can't avoid studying logic . . . It is the basis for all other studies. It is the basis for all math and science. Even music, from Bach to the Beach Boys, is based on logic. Without it, there could be no rational discussion of anything; writing would be impossible. How can you put a sentence together without logical order?
>
> Even interpretation requires logic. We have to assume that the author tried to communicate a logical thought, and

> the only way we have to find that thought is to put all the clues together and set them in logical order. This is as true for English literature as for Bible study . . . Giving a reason for your faith would be useless if it were not a logical reason that you expected others to accept on rational grounds. The only way to avoid logic is to quit thinking, because logic is the basis for all thought (13).

J. M. Robertson has written:

> I would have you realize very clearly that all discussion, all criticism, whether wise or unwise, is reasoning. The blunderers who warn you against reason are simply bad or temporarily confused reasoners. There is no getting away from reasoning, save by way of insanity, and insanity simulates the process of reasoning (qtd. in Black 54).

When it comes to determining (1) whether the Bible is true (2) what its message meant to the first recipients and (3) its application to those of us living today, we must use the process of sound reasoning. Let it be emphasized that there simply is no other process we can use to determine these matters. Robbins explained:

> In elementary school, you studied such things as reading, writing, and arithmetic. These subjects are correctly regarded as basic to all further education. One cannot study history, botany, or computers without being able to read. Reading, writing, and arithmetic are the basics, the tools that permit one to study further, and also to drive, to shop, and to get a job.
>
> But could there be something more basic than the three basics? Something so obvious that most people do not see it, let alone study it? What is there in common between calculating, reading, and writing? The answer of course is thought. One must think in order to read and write. Thinking, just as everything else, is supposed to follow certain rules, if we are to think correctly. Sometimes we make mistakes

in thinking. We jump to conclusions; we make unwarranted assumptions; we generalize. There is a subject that catalogues these mistakes, points them out so that we can recognize them in the future, and then explains the rules for avoiding them. That subject is logic (1).

Logic — The *Expression* Of It

The most fundamental expression of the need to be logical in our thinking is the law of rationality. Lionel Ruby wrote, "Every person who is interested in logical thinking accepts what we shall call the 'law of rationality' which may be stated as follows: We ought to justify our conclusions by adequate evidence" (131).

This law, or principle, of rationality, sometimes called the "law of sufficient reason," says one should draw only such conclusions as are warranted by the evidence. This principle is recognized by every rational person whether or not he has formally studied the discipline of Logic. It is a principle which is at work continually in the lives of all sane people. Deaver has explained it in the following:

> For example, suppose that a man tells his wife that he needs to run to town. She wants to know **why**. It will not do for him to say something like, "Well, dogs bark," or "Clouds surely are pretty." If he were to say something like the above, a troubled look would likely appear on his wife's face, and his remark would be interpreted by her as a sign that either (1) he did not really understand her question, or that (2) something is wrong with her husband! We all understand that we constantly are giving **reasons** as explanations for positions we take (conclusions we draw). We also try to give **adequate** ones, not ones that will not stand further investigation. If the husband in our illustration (upon being asked by his wife why he needed to go to town) responded with: "I need to get some gas for the car," he is seeking to explain or justify the position that he has taken (the position was: I need to go to town). He is trying to give an adequate reason for his conclusion. He is reasoning. He is being logical (132).

One might attempt to deny the need to honor the law of rationality, but the very moment he begins to give reasons for denying this law he is, in fact, admitting the truth of it. The very fact that one would ask, "How do we know it is true that we ought to justify our conclusions by adequate evidence?," is proof that this law or principle is true. One who asks for such is calling for the sufficient evidence that warrants the conclusion: One ought to justify his conclusions by sufficient evidence.

The Bible honors the law of rationality. The following biblical statement illustrates something very crucial in reference to the hermeneutic of the apostles: "And according to Paul's custom, he went to them, and for three sabbaths reasoned with them from the Scriptures, explaining and giving evidence . . ." (Acts 17:2-3, NASV). This biblical passage is of value in identifying something very crucial about the basic approach of the apostles toward the Bible and the interpretation and proclamation of its message. Note that Paul reasoned (***dialegomai***) from the scriptures. The example of Paul (as well as the example of those who heard Paul–Acts 17:11) shows that the apostles honored the law of rationality in their handling of the scriptures and enjoined such on their auditors (cf. 1 Thess. 5:21; 1 Pet. 3:15; 2 Pet. 1:16-21; 1 John 4:1).

The relationship of the law of rationality to the process of biblical hermeneutics has been well summarized by Thomas B. Warren:

> . . . In order to properly interpret the Bible, one must both *recognize* (understand) and *honor* (by using it correctly) the law of rationality, which says that one should draw only such conclusions as are warranted by the evidence. This involves a careful *gathering of the evidence* which is relevant to a particular problem, recognizing that the evidence involves both the "immediate context" (what comes just *before* and just *after* the statement which is under consideration) and the "remote context" (whatever else the *entire Bible* has to say that is *truly relevant* to the problem under consideration). Then, having determined the material which comprises both the "immediate context" and the "remote context," one must recognize that composite as the "total context." Then, having

> determined the "total context" (recognizing that to be the *total evidence*), one must then *correctly handle* that evidence. This means that, recognizing the law of rationality (and, thus, drawing only such conclusions as are warranted by the evidence), one will use the laws of logic (the principles of valid reasoning) in order to ascertain when conclusions *are* warranted and when they are *not* warranted) (Logic v).

Logic — The *Essentiality* Of It

In response to Festus' charge: "Paul, you are out of your mind! Your great learning is driving you made" (Acts 26:24, NASV), Paul said, "I am not out of my mind, most excellent Festus, but I utter words of sober truth" (NASV).

Both preceding and following this statement, Paul referred to the Scriptures (Acts 26:22, 27). The New American Standard Version footnote on Acts 26:25 says, "Lit., of truth and rationality." On the word ***sophrosyne*** (rationality) the *Theological Dictionary of the New Testament* states:

> Lexicographically one can only describe its meaning by certain catchwords. It denotes a. "the rational" in the sense of what is intellectually sound . . . It then denotes b. "rational" without illusion . . . The ref. here is. . . simply to "being rational"... (Luck 1097).

This significant statement made by the apostle Paul powerfully shows the essential place of logic (sound reasoning) in the hermeneutic of Paul and the other apostles of Jesus Christ. Paul was concerned about being intellectually sound (i.e. honoring the law of rationality and reasoning correctly).

To be logical with regard to the Bible means to correctly infer what the explicit statements of the Bible imply. The *explicit* teaching of the Bible is that which the Bible teaches in so many words. It is that which is directly stated. For example, the statement "except one be born of water and spirit, he cannot enter into the kingdom of God" is *explicitly* stated in the American Standard Version of the Bible in John 3:5. In contrast, the statement, "No one can enter the church which Jesus bought with His own blood, without being baptized in the name of Jesus Christ for the remission of sins" is not *explicitly* stated in the Bible but it is taught implicitly (i.e. it is deduced [inferred] from what is *explicitly* stated).

Understanding that (1) the Bible teaches both explicitly and implicitly and (2) correct interpretation of the Bible involves reasoning correctly by inferring what the explicit statements of the Bible imply are two absolute essentials for a proper hermeneutic. Warren stated:

> . . . The Bible itself demands that it be studied carefully, systematically, and prayerfully. This means: (1) that the evidence (as to what the Bible actually says **explicitly**) must be gathered (learned) and (2) that the one who has gathered the evidence must then **handle** that evidence correctly (that is, in harmony with the principles of valid reasoning). It is not sufficient to merely learn that the Bible **explicitly** says thus and so. It is conceivable that one could even **memorize the entire Bible** and yet **not understand** what the Bible actually teaches. This author has studied a number of years in denominational seminaries and universities under professors who were experts in biblical languages and who knew what the Bible **explicitly** says almost from cover to cover. Yet, not a single one of them even understood the plan of salvation which is set out in the Bible. And, not a single one of them understood what the Bible teaches about the one true church. On and on we could go about their ignorance of what the Bible really teaches — what it **means** by what it **says**. Why is this the case? Why did these men, who were so learned in what the Bible **explicitly says**, know so little as to what the Bible **actually teaches**? They have exactly the same set of explicit statements (of the Bible) which we do. They have the same explicit statements in Hebrew, in Greek, and in English. I repeat: if inferring what is implied by the explicit statements of the Bible can lead only to mere **human** doctrine (which cannot be bound on anyone as the will of God)–which the irrationalists claim–then all any of us could do, in "preaching" God's word would

be to merely **read** the Bible, making no comment at all (for all of our comments, given the erroneous view of the **irrationalists**, would have to be inferences which, given their theory, could be nothing more than **mere human doctrines** which could never be bound on anyone).

Why do Baptists, for example, who have the same explicit Bible statements which we have, teach so strongly that men are saved from sin at the point of faith, before and without being baptized in the name of Christ? There is one reason why they do such: They do not **infer** the **conclusions** which are **implied** by the **explicit statements** of the Bible! That is the whole matter in a "nutshell!" It is true that they draw inferences (that is, they draw conclusions), but they draw the **wrong** conclusions. They draw conclusions which are **not warranted** by the explicit statements of the Bible.

Why do "Pentecostals", who have the same **explicit** Bible statements which we have, teach so strongly that some men living today actually have the same miraculous gifts of the Holy Spirit which the apostles and prophets in the early church had? There is one reason they do such: They do **not infer** the **conclusions** which are **implied** by the **explicit** statements of the Bible! As do the Baptists, the "Pentecostals" draw inferences (that is, they draw conclusions) from the **explicit** statements of the Bible, but they do not **infer** the conclusions which are actually **implied** by the explicit statements of the Bible. And why do they draw the wrong conclusions? Because they **do not reason** correctly about the explicit statements of the Bible. They make logical errors in considering the explicit statements of the Bible. Anyone who formulates fallacious arguments in regard to the explicit statements of the Bible will not learn the truth about whatever biblical topic is being considered.

Why do the "Jehovah's Witnesses", who at least have access to the same **explicit** statements of the Bible which we have, teach so strongly that Jesus of Nazareth was nothing

> more than a created being? They teach this ungodly doctrine because they have **inferred** a conclusion which is **not implied** by the explicit statements of the Bible.
>
> This procedure could be carried on to the consideration of the hundreds of religious groups in the world which claim to be followers of the Lord Jesus Christ. In each, the errors which they espouse can be rightly attributed to the fact that they infer conclusions which are not **implied** by the explicit statements of the Bible.
>
> I want to make clear that various factors can be involved as to **why** these various groups draw these false conclusions from the explicit statements of the Bible. For example, one might have been misled into accepting an erroneous principle of reasoning, or one may be so determined to hold to a certain viewpoint that he simply will not let himself see the true implications of biblical statements, or one may. . . come to the point that he simply rejects the role of valid reasoning in biblical hermeneutics and, thus, pay no attention to the way he himself reasons (*Logic* 15-17).

The advocates of the new hermeneutic deny the role of deduction (inferring what the explicit statements imply) in interpreting the Bible. In so doing they are self contradictory for they deduce, and bind their deduction, that deductions are not binding when it comes to interpreting the Bible. They try to show how "logical" it is that we should not depend on logic when concerned with hermeneutics. They "reason" that one does not need reason in interpreting the Bible. All of this reminds one of the philosopher's observation that no one ever turned against reason until reason turned against him or, as another has suggested, that no one ever tried to break logic but what logic broke him (Carnell 492).

Such statements as the following manifest a crucial misunderstanding with regard to hermeneutics generally, and with regard to the role of logic in hermeneutics specifically:

> The problem with necessary inference is that we cannot prove absolutely whether a given inference is even logically correct,

> let alone necessary. . . . We must be tolerant of what other people think on subjects not explicitly dealt with by the Bible . . . .
>
> We must learn to "agree to disagree" about doctrines not explicitly taught by the Word. Only direct statements tell us for certain what God thinks. "Necessary" inferences tell us only what men think (Nutter 44-45).

Given the above theory, viz. that "only direct (*explicit*) statements tell us for certain what God thinks," no one could ever prove that there is even a single instruction in the Bible which is binding on anyone today. Such is the case because there are no *explicit* instructions in the Bible directed to anyone on Earth today. Therefore, it must be the case that the only way one can determine whether a verse in the Bible applies to him today would be through inferring (deducing) what the explicit statements of the Bible imply.

If it is the case that "only direct statements tell us for certain what God thinks" then the position itself (viz. that only direct statements tell us for certain what God thinks) must be rejected, because there is *no* direct statement in the Bible which so instructs men. The position is self-contradictory, and is thus false. Where is the direct statement which teaches that matters which require man to use reason (i.e. logic) must be regarded as non-binding? Where is *even one* direct statement in the Bible which can be shown to be directed to anyone now living on Earth without correctly using deduction (correctly inferring what the explicit statements imply)?

Conclusion

In order to properly interpret the Scriptures one must honor the law of rationality. In order to understand the Bible one must not only learn what the Bible says *explicitly*, but having learned this (what the explicit statements are), he must correctly handle (reason correctly) these explicit statements which means he must correctly infer (i.e. reason correctly) what the explicit statements imply. As Warren put it:

It must be re-emphasized that all men, having been created by God with intelligent minds (able to recognize, to observe and to properly consider the evidence which God has given) are required by God to draw only such conclusions as are warranted by the evidence . . . . logical reasoning is not the answer to everything. Logic is **necessary** to a proper life, but **logic alone** is certainly **not sufficient** for such a life. Correct **reasoning** has its place and so does **emotion**. But both reasoning and emotion must be given **content** by the revelation of God, the Bible (Jer. 10:23; 2 Tim. 3:16-17). No purely **intellectual** life can be adequate any more than can a purely **emotional** one. Both are necessary, but both also need **revelation** from God (*Example* 31).

Works Cited:

Black, Max . *Critical Thinking.* 1946. Englewood Cliffs: Prentice Hall, 1952.

Carnell, Edward John. *A Philosophy of The Christian Religion,* Grand Rapids: Wm. B. Eerdmans Publishing Co., 1954.

Collier, Gary. *Bringing The Word to Life: As Assessment of the Hermeneutical Impasse in Churches of Christ.* Christian Scholars' Conference Paper. Pepperdine University, July 1988.

Deaver, Mac. "The Necessity of Logic in Rightly Dividing The Word". *General Hermeneutics, The Fourth Annual Shenandoah Lectures.* San Antonio: Shenandoah Church of Christ,1990.

Downs, Douglas. *The Future of Restorationist Hermeneutics.* Christian Scholars' Conference Paper. Pepperdine University, July 1988.

Geisler, Norman L. and Ronald M. Brooks. *Come Let Us Reason.* Grand Rapids: Baker Book House, 1990.

Luck, Ulrich. *Theological Dictionary of the New Testament.* 1971. Vol. 7. Grand Rapids: Wm. B. Eerdmans, 1978. 10 vols.

Nutter, Mark. "Necessary Inference and the Limitations of Logic". *The Gospel Advocate* 132 (1990) : 44.

Robbins, John W. "Why Study Logic?". *The Trinity Review.* No. 44 July/August 1985.

Ruby, Lionel. *Logic An Introduction.* Chicago: J. P. Lippincott Company, 1960.

Warren, Thomas B. *Logic And The Bible.* Jonesboro: National Christian Press, 1982.

Warren, Thomas B. *When is an Example Binding*? Jonesboro: National Christian Press, 1975.

CHAPTER 4

BALANCING EMOTION AND REASON

One of life's greatest challenges is the challenge to develop a balanced life. A lack of balance results in all kinds of problems in various areas of life. However, proper balance results in many positives. Balance of color and sound can bring beauty to art and music. Balance of diet is vital to the health of the physical body.

Balance is essential to true religion. The history of religion involves a study of action, reaction, and extremes which often show imbalance. One of the specific areas where such extremism (imbalance) often has been seen is in the area of the intellect (reason) and the emotions. We often see a wide range of religious thinking and expression which runs from cold intellectualism to impassioned emotionalism. Man is both an intellectual and emotional being. However, there must be a proper balance between these two vital parts of man. As we attempt to discover the proper balance between reason and emotion in religion we will do such in view of three areas of consideration: (1) a ***definition*** of the terms, (2) a ***description*** of the problem, and (3) a ***declaration*** of the truth.

Definition of the Terms

Emotion involves "excitement, state of feeling" (Webster

372). Feeling can be a powerful motivation. When Peter set forth evidence on the Day of Pentecost which demanded the conclusion, "Therefore let all the house if Israel know assuredly that God has made this Jesus, who you crucified, both Lord and Christ" (Acts 2:36), it stirred his hearers very deeply. "Now, when they heard this, they were cut to the heart, and said to Peter and the rest of the apostles, 'Men and brethren what shall we do?' " (Acts 2:37). *Cut* (pricked, KJV) means, "be pierced, stabbed. . . the feeling of sharp pain connected with anxiety, remorse, etc." (Arndt and Gingrich 416). Thayer says it means "to pain the mind sharply, agitate it vehemently: used especially of the emotion of sorrow" (334-35). The gospel appeals to the emotions of man. Just *knowing* the truth is not enough. Man must be moved to obey the truth. His emotions must be moved. He must act upon what he has heard. When the intellect (reason) has been reached with the facts, and the emotions stirred, the volition (will) must be activated. One may have his intellect (reason) addressed, and his emotions stirred, but his will may not be activated (cf. Acts 24:25).

Reason is the power of comprehending, inferring, or thinking in rational ways. To be rational is to honor the law of rationality. This law, or principle, of rationality, sometimes called the law of sufficient reason, says one should draw only such conclusions as are warranted by the evidence. This principle is recognized by every rational person whether or not he has formally studied the discipline of Logic. It is a principle which is at work continually in the lives of all sane people. As I have stated elsewhere (see chapter Three: *Logic, Reason, And The Bible*), one might attempt to deny the need to honor the law of rationality, but the very moment he begins to give reasons for denying this law he is, in fact, admitting the truth of it.

Description Of The Problem

The challenge of properly balancing emotion and reason in religion involves overcoming the extremes of (1) throwing the intellect (reason) into neutral while the emotions take over and run wild and/or (2) laying aside the emotions with the result being a cold, heartless religion. In order to possess the biblical balance of emotion and reason, the following principles must be acknowledged:

1. *There is a place for tears in religion.* Jesus wept (Luke 19:41; John 11:35; Heb. 5:7). The psalmist confessed that "rivers of water run down from my eyes, because men do not keep Your law" (Psalm 119:136). The apostle Paul preached with tears (Acts 20:31). As he wrote to the Philippians, he did so "even weeping" (Philip. 3:18). The prophet Jeremiah desired a head full of waters, and eyes that were a fountain of tears, that he might weep day and night for his people (Jer. 9:1). It could be that some of us who preach have been so careful to avoid emotionalism that we have gone to the opposite extreme and have lost passion in our preaching, and we have become as cold as icicles.

2. *There is a place for enthusiasm in religion.* Enthusiasm is "strong excitement of feeling; ardor; something inspiring zeal or fervor; passion" (Webster 381). The biblical word is *zeal.* Although zeal is not sufficient, it is essential (John 2:13-17; Rom. 12:11; Titus 2:11-14). Enthusiasm is not a superficial kind of showmanship. It is the spiritual product of "God within us" (***en*** plus ***theos***). Our singing should be spirited, joyous, and hearty (Col. 3:16, 23). Our response to the preaching of the Word of God should be one of zeal and enthusiasm (cf. Acts 17:11; Jer. 15:16). This beautiful balance of reason (understanding) and emotion (joy and feeling) is observed in the following:

> And Ezra opened the book in the sight of all the people, for he was standing above all the people; and when he opened it, all the people stood up. And Ezra blessed the Lord, the great God. Then all the people answered, "Amen, Amen!" while lifting up their hands. And they bowed their heads and worshipped the Lord with their faces to the ground.... So they read distinctly from the book, in the Law of God, and they gave the sense, and helped them to understand the reading. . . . Then he said to them. . . the joy of the Lord is your strength. . . And all the people went their way to eat and drink to send portions and REJOICE GREATLY, BECAUSE THEY UNDERSTOOD THE WORDS that were declared to them (Neh. 8:5-6, 8, 10, 12, caps mine, CCP III).

3. *There is a law of succession in mental states - - knowing (intellectual), feeling (emotion) and willing (volitional).* Everest made a great observation, which evinces the beautiful balance of the Christian system, when he stated:

> Knowing is the basis of emotional excitement; and both knowing and feeling must precede willing or choice. The apostles were sent first to turn men from darkness to light, to make known the great facts of the gospel. Preaching the word and thorough instruction were to precede all else. The feelings were to be aroused and kindled into godly sorrow by the nature of the gospel facts; facts. . . finely adapted to produce this result. . . (186).

No inspired writer ever sought to arouse the emotions until he had first presented the facts of the gospel sustained by adequate evidence. Emotions move one to do what is right. Emotions do not determine what is right. People can be moved by emotion to believe the erroneous and do what is wrong, even with great sincerity. Such is one of the tragedies of denominationalism and other departures from historic Christianity.

Declaration Of The Truth

Some years ago a speaker at a college lectureship stated: "There's more to life than logic. . . . And life is not logical. There's an emotional element in Christianity and for us to try to construct a system which includes all the elements in some kind of rational or logical way is to misunderstand part of what life is all about."

The above statement implies that there are various "elements" in Christianity, one of which is emotion; i.e. "There's an emotional element in Christianity." Furthermore, the statement says that to have a system where "all the elements" are included in a "rational or logical way is to misunderstand part of what life is all about." To this we would raise the following crucial questions: (1) Is the logical (rational) nature of Christianity just an element of Christianity as is the emotional? (2) Is the system to which the speaker referred the Christian system? (3) If the system does not include *all* its elements in a "rational or logical way," does this mean then that *a part* of the Christian system is irrational and illogical? (4) If a part of the Christian system is irrational and illogical, then is it not the case that Christianity is based on insufficient evidence?

The truth of the matter is that every religion available to man has an emotional element within it (Christianity included). However, it is not the emotional element of Christianity which proves that Christianity is the one true religion. I know the Christian religion is the one true religion, but not because it makes me feel good. The Muslim, Buddhist, denominationalist, atheist (and others) may each feel very good, but this is not sufficient evidence to warrant the conclusion that one's religion is true. It is whether a religion honors the law of rationality which determines whether that religion is the true religion. Only *one* religion honors the law of rationality (i.e. only one religion acts in harmony with the demand to justify its claims by sufficient evidence) and that is Christianity. To be rational means that one will draw only such conclusions as are warranted by the evidence.

Although it is the case that a vital part of man is his emotions, and in a wonderful way a part of Christianity appeals to his emotions (Philip. 4:4,7; 1 Pet. 1:8,9; John 16:33; et al), *no man ever has the right to be irrational in any part of religion* (i.e. no man ever has the right to espouse a position for which he does not have sufficient evidence) and no part of Christianity, whether it be emotional, intellectual, or spiritual, teaches that man can refuse to be rational (i.e. refuse to justify his conclusions by adequate evidence) and be right in so doing. The Bible demands that logic (sound reasoning) be honored in all things (1 Thess. 5:21). ***WHEN ANY PART OF RELIGION IS SET AGAINST LOGIC (SOUND REASONING) THE RESULT IS THE LOSS OF A TEST FOR TRUTH AND ERROR.***

Conclusion

Christianity is the one true religion and is therefore the only religion which properly balances emotion and reason. There is no contradiction between emotion and reason in biblical Christianity. The faithful Christian life is one in which "you rejoice with joy inexpressible and full of glory" (1 Pet. 1:8), and yet it is a life in which one is to "always be ready to give a defense to everyone who asks you a reason for the hope that is in you" (1 Pet. 3:15). The conversion of the treasurer of Ehtiopia (Acts 8:26-39) provides insight and understanding into the proper balance of emotion and reason in religion. When the preacher, Philip, encountered the Ethiopian he asked, "Do you understand what you are reading?" (Acts 8:30). Here is the appeal to the intellect (reason and understanding). Philip explained the biblical material to the Ethiopian man. We see here that Christianity is first an *intellectual* experience (i.e. understanding, reasoning, thinking, and knowing). After he learned the meaning of the Bible, and understood its implications for his life, the Ethiopian wanted to obey. **CORRECT REASONING WILL LEAD TO CORRECT CONCLUSIONS TO WHICH ONE'S WILL MUST SUBMIT**. And so, the man was baptized (Acts 8:36-38). It was following this rational understanding of the will of God, coupled with the decision to obey this will, and doing just this, that "he went on his way rejoicing" (Acts 8:39). Great human emotion was evident, but it was the result of the proper application of the principles of sound reasoning. The biblical order is (1) ***FACTS***, (2) ***FAITH***, and (3) ***FEELING***.

Franklin Camp once offered a wonderful summation of the need to balance emotion and reason. He stated:

> In order for one to understand the gospel, he must be taught and, when properly taught, if he can be reached at all, the story of sin and the cross of Christ will touch the deepest emotions of the heart and lead the will to loving submission to truth. When one is a Christian, there is a constant thrill of undying gratitude that keeps aglow the warmth of the Christian love and sends one singing on his way in service to God and man. This is Christianity. It is neither the formal and cold religion that leaves one indifferent and unconcerned, nor is it characterized by wild, emotional scenes that have no regard for truth.
>
> Let us be careful and be sure that our Christianity is based upon a Bible instructed intellect and emotions that respond to the greatest story that has ever fallen upon the ears of

man. May this produce within each of us a love and response to the love of God and a gratitude that will keep us happy. Rejoicing on our way as we serve both God and man (4).

Works Cited:

Arndt, William F. and Wilbur F. Gingrich. *A Greek-English Lexicon of the New Testament and Other Early Christian Literature.* 1957. Chicago: U Chicago P, 1973.

Camp, Franklin. "A Balanced Life." *The Word of Life.* 6.3 (1977) : 1-4.

Everest, Harvey W. *The Divine Demonstration. A Text-Book of Christian Evidence.* 1884. Nashville: Gospel Advocate, 1972.

Thayer, Joseph Henry. *Greek-English Lexicon of the New Testament.* 1962. Grand Rapids: Zondervan, 1973.

Webster's New Collegiate Dictionary. Springfield: G&C Merriam Company, 1974.

CHAPTER 5

THE CONFIRMATION OF THE WORD

> . . . And these signs shall accompany them that believe: in my name shall they cast out demons; they shall speak with new tongues; they shall take up serpents, and if they drink any deadly thing it shall in no wise hurt them; they shall lay hands on the sick and they shall recover.
>
> So then the Lord Jesus, after he had spoken unto them, was received up into heaven, and at down at the right hand of God. And they went forth, and preached everywhere, the Lord working with them, and confirming the word by the signs that followed. Amen (Mark 16:17-20, ASV).

The above verses have been a textual and doctrinal battleground for centuries. Set in the context of the post-resurrection appearances of Jesus (Mark 16:1-13), i.e. "after he was risen" (Mark 16:14), and connected with the assignment of the Great Commission (Mark 16:15-16), it should come as no surprise that the authenticity of this crucial text has often been challenged. For the purposes of this study, the authenticity of this text as a part of the sacred canon, is assumed. However, that these verses, and the others that compose the so-called "long ending" of Mark's gospel account, are genuine, has been unequivocally proved to be the case. See the following: Varner, W. Terry, "Is Mark 16:9-20 Fraudulent or Genuine?", *2001 West Virginia School of Preaching Lectureship*; Burgon, John W., *The Last Twelve Verses Of The Gospel According To St. Mark,* Reprint: Faith and Facts Press, n.d.; *Warren-Ballard Debate On The Plan Of Salvation,* Jonesboro, AR: National Christian Press, Inc., 3rd Printing, 1979.

The conclusion of the erudite Bible scholar, J.W. McGarvey, is that with which I concur:

> Our final conclusion is, that the passage in question is authentic in all its details, and that there is no reason to doubt that it was written by the same hand which indited the proceeding parts of this narrative. The objections which have been raised against it are better calculated to shake our confidence in Biblical Criticism than in genuineness of this inestimable portion of the word of God (382).

Jesus was the speaker of the words that compose verses seventeen and eighteen. However, there is no identification of the place where these words were spoken. It may be the case that these words were spoken during a post-resurrection appearance in Galilee (cf. Matt. 26:32; 28:7, 16-20; Mark 14:28; 16:7, 14-18). They may parallel the Great Commission account of Matthew, but it is not certain that such is the case. In fact, a case can be made that these words of Jesus recorded by Mark were spoken on a different occasion than that referred to in Matthew 28:16-20, since the Matthew account identifies the place as "the mountain" in Galilee (Matt. 28:16), and Mark's account refers to when "they sat at meat" (Mark 16:14).

In addition to the occasion when the words of verses seventeen and eighteen were spoken, this text also involves the occasion of the ascension (verse 19; cf. Acts 1:8-11) which took place on Mount Olivet (Acts 1:12). The text states: "So then the Lord Jesus after he had spoken unto them (i.e. after he had spoken to them for forty days following the resurrection–Acts 1:3), was received up into heaven. . ." (Mark 16:19). Verse nineteen begins a new paragraph in the English Bible. The occasion with which verse nineteen in concerned is to be distinguished from that of verse eighteen. Therefore, the following conclusions may be drawn with regard to the context of Mark 16:17-20:

1. Verses seventeen and eighteen were spoken during a specific post-resurrection appearance.
2. The former part of verse nineteen may be a reference to the entire forty day period when Jesus had spoken to the apostles (Acts 1:3).
3. The latter part of verse nineteen is a reference to the ascension, which occurred on Mount Olivet on the final day of the above-mentioned forty-day period (Acts 1:8-12).
4. The passage concludes with a kind of summation of the Acts of the Apostles which shows how "they went forth, and preached everywhere, the Lord working with them, and confirming the word by the signs that followed" (Mark 16:20).

Affirmation Of The Text

The basic affirmation of this text is: "And these signs shall accompany them that believe. . ." (Mark 16:17). Literally, "these are the signs which shall follow." *Signs* (***semeia***, nom. acc. pl. of ***semeion***) was used to refer to "the sign or distinguishing mark by which something is known" (Arndt and Gingrich 755). Paul used the term to refer to "the token in every epistle" he wrote to mark its genuineness (2 Thess. 3:17), and the "wonders or miracles" (755) performed by a true apostle to identify him as such (2 Cor. 12:12). The word occurs twice in the text before us (verses 17, 20). It refers here to ". . . a wonder or miracle, an event that is contrary to the usual course of nature. . . miracle of divine origin, performed by God himself. . ." (755) ***Semeion*** (sign) appears seventy-seven times in the New Testament (Gospels: 48 times; Acts: 13 times; Epistles of Paul: 8 times; Hebrews: 1 time; Revelation: 7 times). A few passages for consideration in which the word is found include John 2:23; 3:2; 20:30-31; Acts 2:22, 43; Heb. 2:4. Ancient Papyri have been cited that establish the idea of "proof" as the meaning of ***semeion***

(Moulton and Milligan 573). The term involves the "things which God did to accredit the preaching which began with the proclamation of the Lord" (Rengstorf 260). [NOTE: The reader is referred to an in-depth study of ***semeion*** in the preceding source, 200-269]. The basic meaning of ***semeion*** is "a sign. . . by which one recognizes a particular person or thing, a confirmatory, corroborative, authenticating mark or token" (Hofius 626). These signs are ***evidences*** intended to prove that the gospel of Christ and the claims therein are true. The implication of this text is that Christianity honors the law of rationality which states that one ought to draw only such conclusions as are warranted by the evidence. The Christian faith is rational. It sustains the truth of its claims through the framework of sufficient evidence (Luke 1:1-4; John 20:30-31; Acts 26:25; Rom. 1:18-20; 1 Thess. 5:21; 1 Pet. 3:15, et. al).

The charismatic movement, and other subjective religious movements such as latter-day revelation claimants (Mormons, etc.), often run to Mark 16:17-20 in an attempt to defend their claims of present-day tongue speaking, miraculous healings, etc. However, when the passage is exegeted accurately, and understood, it is not seen as a place of refuge for subjective religious viewpoints and practices which deny the law of rationality. Rather, this text makes a great affirmation of how Christian faith is rational, i.e. it establishes its claims by adequate evidence. Thus, it addresses one of the great needs in religion, viz. the recognition of the essentiality of reasoning correctly in order to arrive at the truth. One must gather the evidence, reason correctly with regard to that evidence, and draw only such conclusions as are warranted by the evidence (cf. John 3:2; John 20:30-31). However, as one writer has shown, so much in religion today fails at this point:

> Lamentably, irrationalism has greatly affected the visible church. The Charismatic movement is just one example of this. The primacy of the intellect and of truth has been replaced with emotionalism, ecstatic utterances, incoherent experiences, and anti-doctrinal statements (e.g. "give me Jesus, not exegesis"). Faith has nothing to do with thought, let alone logic. All too frequently we encounter what Ronald Nash referred to as "the religious revolt against logic" (Crampton 2-3).

The affirmation of Mark 16:17-20 is that these signs would accompany ***(parakoloutheo)***, follow closely, characterize (Bagster 304), ". . . attend those who have come to believe" (Arndt and Gingrich 624), or "follow along the side" (Rienecker 135). The signs would follow "them that believe" ***(tauta pisteusasin)***. The signs would follow (accompany, follow closely, follow along the side) ***them*** (plural) that believe. Believe is an aorist participle. The "having believed" ones would have the signs follow alongside of them. McGarvey explained it in the following:

> The promise is, not that these signs shall follow for any specified time, NOR THAT THEY SHOULD FOLLOW EACH INDIVIDUAL BELIEVER, but merely that THEY SHALL FOLLOW AND FOLLOW "THE BELIEVERS" TAKEN AS A BODY. They did follow the believers during the apostolic age - not every individual believer, but all, or nearly all, the organized bodies of the believers. This was a complete fulfillment of what was promised. He who claims that the promise included more than this, presses the words of the promise beyond what is necessary to a full realization of their meaning. . . (375, caps mine, CCPIII).

Classification Of The Signs

The signs (evidence, proof) that would accompany (follow alongside) them that believe are as follows: ". . . in my name shall they cast out demons; they shall speak with new tongues; they shall take up serpents, and if they drink any deadly thing it shall in no wise hurt them; they shall lay hands on the sick and they shall recover" (verse 17-18). Jesus promised five signs that would accompany the body of believers:

1. The power to expel demons.
2. The ability to speak in new tongues.
3. The ability to pick up serpents, that is, to pick up venomous snakes without being physically harmed.

4. The gift of being able to drink deadly poison without being hurt.
5. The power to lay hands on the sick, who will then recover.

Each of these five signs can be classified in one of the areas of the miraculous gifts of the Holy Spirit that Paul set forth (1 Cor. 12:8-11). These signs can be classified as follows:

1. The power to expel demons is a manifestation of the gift of "working of miracles" (1 Cor. 12:10).
2. The ability to speak in new tongues is equivalent to the gift of "diverse kinds of tongues" (1 Cor. 12:10).
3. The ability to pick up serpents without being harmed and/or drinking deadly poison without being hurt are also manifestations of the gift of "workings of miracles" (1 Cor. 12:10).
4. The power to lay hands on the sick so that they then recover is a manifestation of "gifts of healings" (1 Cor. 12:9).

These miraculous gifts of the Holy Spirit were imparted to believers in the first century church through "the laying on of the apostles' hands" (Acts 8:14-19). There were signs ***(semeia)*** that followed alongside the apostles as evidence that they were genuine, and to prove that what they were preaching was the true revelation of God (2 Cor. 12:12; Acts 2:43). However, it is also the case that those upon whom the apostles laid their hands, in order to impart the Holy Spirit in a miraculous measure, were also able to perform various signs as evidence to confirm the word they preached (cf. Acts 8:4-7, 14-21).

Jesus said, "In my name. . ." (***en to onomati mou***). To do something "in the name of" another can mean "to do a thing, i.e. by one's command and authority, acting on his behalf, promoting his cause" (Thayer 447). It can mean "in the power of . . . in acknowledgement or confession of... in recognition of the authority of (sometimes combined with the thought of relying or resting on)" (Vine, Vol. 3 100).

"Shall cast out demons" (verse 17) is from ***daimonia***

ekbalousin. It means to drive out, or expel, demons or evil spirits (cf. Mark 1:34, 39, 43; 3:15, 23; 6:13; 7:26; 9:18, 28; 16:9).

"They shall speak with new tongues" (verse 17) is translated from ***glossais*** (tongues) ***lalesousin*** (they shall speak) and ***kainais*** (new). ***Glossa*** is a language (Arndt and Gingrich 161). It refers to "a tongue, i.e. the language used by a particular people in distinction from that of other nations" (Thayer 118).

The second chapter of Acts provides divine commentary on what is meant by "new tongues". As Vine has affirmed:

> "The new tongues", ***kainos***, of Mark 16:17 are the "other tongues", ***heteros***, of Acts 2:4. These languages, however, were "new" and "different", not in the sense that they had never been heard before, or that they were new to the hearers, for it is plain from v. 8 that this is not the case; they were new languages to the speaker, different from those in which they were accustomed to speak (Vol. 3 109).

"They shall speak with new tongues" consisted of speaking real, intelligible languages–the miracle being that those who spoke in these "new tongues" had never learned (studied) these languages prior to fluently speaking them.

"They shall take up serpents, and if they drink any deadly thing it will not hurt them..." (verse 18) consists of two statements conjoined by ***kan*** (and if). ***Arousin*** (take up) can mean to "take up, lift, raise, bear, carry, take away, remove, destroy, kill" (Bagster 9) or "pick up" (Arndt and Gingrich 23). Jesus sent seventy disciples by twos into every city and place where He was about to come (Luke 10:1), and He gave them "authority to tread upon serpents and scorpions... so that nothing shall in any wise hurt you" (Luke 10:19). Paul was unharmed by a serpent at Melita (Acts 28:3ff). This incident may, or may not, be a direct illustration of Mark 16:18. However, it surely belongs to this class of ***semeia*** (signs.)

On December 6-9, 1976, Alan E. Highers debated Raymond G. Bishop at Ripley, Mississippi. Bishop represented the Pentecostal Oneness doctrine advocated by such denominations as the United Pentecostal Church. He contended that all five of the miraculous gifts of Mark 16:17-18 are still in effect. On the third night of the debate, Highers affirmed: "The Scriptures teach that the Holy Spirit baptism with the signs and miracles ceased by the time the complete will of God was revealed and confirmed or by the end of the apostolic age." He made the argument that the miracles of the first century cannot be duplicated today, and that they ceased when the New Testament was fully delivered and sufficiently confirmed. It was on this third night of the debate that Highers delivered one of his most devastating blows against Pentecostal doctrinal error. He presented a western diamond-back rattlesnake, approximately four feet long, in full possession of his venom. As the rattling of this venomous creature was heard throughout all parts of the large auditorium a quiet hush came over the audience. Both Bishop and his moderator were "visibly shaken" by the snake. Even a child could see that Bishop dared not "take up serpents" as per his contention on Mark 16:17-18 (Elkins 26-27).

"... And if they drink any deadly thing, it shall in no wise hurt them" (verse 18). The word translated *deadly* is ***thanasimon***. It means "fatal" (Bagster 195). *Hurt*, or *harm*, is from ***blaphei*** (*fut. active ind. of* ***blapto***) and means to weaken, hurt, harm, or injure (Bagster 70). We have no example of this specific sign in the New Testament. However, tradition reports that the apostle John drank poison without harm (Lenski 769). Some presume to know what is said here about venomous serpents and poisonous drink is a journey "into the twilight of apocryphal story." To this presumption, Lenski has responded in the following manner:

> ... Is it really a small thing, something fanciful and apocryphal to escape sudden death by venom or poisonous drink? Is healing the sick like Peter's mother-in-law from a fever so much greater as a sign, so much less apocryphal than to escape mortal dangers? The exegete should always keep his balance.
>
> To prefer the charge of being apocryphal against this section of Mark's Gospel is ineffective because it could be launched only against the serpents and the drink. The demons, tongues, and sick appear too often and at too great length to be included in such a charge. Must all these verses

> from nine to twenty come from a late writer because of these two points? The contrary seems reasonable, namely that no man would have added a word about serpents or poisonous drink if he had undertaken to write a conclusion to Mark's Gospel; only the original writer, Mark himself, dared to add items that are not presented elsewhere. Mark had received them from Peter, and finding fault with them is not good... We have no compilation here, the text, v. 17, 18, stands undisputed, the support for the five items is the same. Therewith let us be content (779).

"... They shall lay hands on the sick and they shall recover" (verse 18). Literally, "upon the infirmed they shall lay hands and well they shall be." See instances of this in the Acts of the Apostles (3:6-7, 15, et al).

Preparation For The Signs

"So then the Lord Jesus, after He had spoken unto them, was received up into heaven, and sat down at the right hand of God" (verse 19). Contained in this brief statement is what can be termed a period of preparation for the signs through (1) the instruction of Jesus (2) the ascension of Jesus and (3) the exaltation of Jesus. The phrase "after He had spoken unto them" is inclusive of the forty-day period when Jesus, following His death and resurrection, presented various proofs to the apostles to show that He was actually alive and also appeared to them for the purpose of instructing them regarding "the things concerning the kingdom of God" (Acts 1:2-3).

This preparation for the coming confirmatory signs also included the ascension. He "was received up into heaven." "Received up" is from ***aneleiphthei,*** which is an aorist participle having reference to the one time historical fact of the ascension of the Christ (cf. Luke 9:51). The ascension is given no distinct report by Matthew and John. Mark and Luke are the only two who mention it directly in their gospel accounts. However, it is given additional attention in several great statements in the Acts of the Apostles. Early on, the ascension was preached by the apostles (Acts 2:34). Peter preached "Jesus: whom the heaven must receive" (Acts 3:21). Paul gave a marvelous summation of the "mystery of godliness," which included, "He who was manifested in the flesh, justified in the spirit, seen of angels, preached among the nations, believed on in the world, RECEIVED UP INTO GLORY" (1 Tim. 3:16, caps mine CCP). Peter wrote that "baptism doth also now save us (... the answer of a good conscience toward God) by the resurrection of Jesus Christ: Who is gone into heaven, and is on the right hand of God; angels and authorities and powers being made subject unto Him" (1 Pet. 3:21-22). The writer of The Epistle to the Hebrews stated: "Having then a great high priest, who has passed through the heavens, Jesus the Son of God..." (Heb. 4:14). The ascension is crucially linked to the fulfillment of the promise that the miraculous signs of confirmation would follow alongside the revealed word as it was preached. Paul showed this link when he wrote, "When He ascended on high, He led captivity captive, and gave gifts unto men (...He that descended is the same also that ascended far above all the heavens, that He might fill all things.) And He gave some to be apostles; and some prophets; and some evangelists; and some pastors and teachers..." (Eph. 4:8-11). The ascension was "the designed, understood, and fitting sequel to" the resurrection (Jamieson, Fausset and Brown 4).

The preparation for the signs also included the fact that, as Jesus ascended, "... He sat down at the right hand of God" (verse 19). He was received up into Heaven (ascension of Jesus) AND sat down at the right hand of God (exaltation of Jesus). "The right hand of God" is an anthropomorphitic phrase (i.e. ascribing human characteristics to non-human personages or things). God as a Spirit, has no right or left (literally), nor do the Scriptures ever speak of God's left. The right hand of God in the Scriptures is a synonym for God's majestic omnipotence. Lenski observed, "The right hand of God is His omnipotent majesty... To sit at His right is to exercise that majestic omnipotence most fully" (778). Cf. Deut. 33:2; Heb. 1:3; Mark 12:36; 14:62, et al. When Jesus left Earth He assumed the place of supreme majesty, power, and dominion. And here is a most comforting doctrine in Scripture, viz. that Jesus is at the right hand of God. In days of turmoil, suffering, perplexity, anxiety, and, ultimately, death, we need to see Jesus at the right hand of God! He has won the victory over death and is on the throne (Heb. 10:12-13)! When Stephen received the hateful gnashing of his enemies' teeth, and the brutal stoning of his physical body, he, undaunted and unmoved from an unflinching loyalty to Jesus, "looked up steadfastly into heaven, and saw the glory of God, and Jesus standing on the right hand of God" (Acts 7:55). He said, "Behold I see the heavens opened, and the Son of Man standing on the right hand of God" (Acts 7:56). When the stress, strain, doubt and depression of life threaten to paralyze our energies, oh, how we need, by faith, to see Him there at the right hand of the Majesty on high (Heb. 1:3) where He is to plead our case (Rom. 8:34-39; Heb. 7:25, 8:1; 1 John 2:1)!

The Revelation That Produced The Need For The Signs

"And they went forth and preached everywhere..." They (the apostles) having gone forth preached (3rd person, pl. aorist active indicative of ***kerusso***–to herald) everywhere (***pantachou***–"in all places"–cf. Acts 24:3). Jesus had told them during the forty-day period that they "shall be my witnesses both in Jerusalem, and in all Judea and Samaria, and unto the uttermost part of the earth" (Acts 1:8). They preached by revelation (cf. John 14:26; 16:13; Gal. 1:11-12). Paul wrote:

> ... You have heard of the dispensation of that grace of God which was given me to you-ward; how that by revelation was made known unto me the mystery, as I wrote before in few words, whereby when you read you can perceive my understanding in the mystery of Christ; which in other generations was not made known unto the sons of men, as it has now been revealed unto His holy apostles and prophets in the Spirit... Unto me who am the less than the least of all saints, was this grace given, to preach unto the Gentiles the unsearchable riches of Christ... (Eph. 3:2-5, 8, ASV).

Where there is new revelation, there must be **confirmation** of that new revelation. Herein lies one of the keys in answering the question of the duration of the confirmatory signs. How long did these signs last? Just as long as the process of new revelation lasted! If there are confirmatory signs today, then new revelation is being given today. However, it is false that new revelation is being given today (John 16:13; 1 Cor. 13:8-10; Jude 3; Rev. 22:18-19). Therefore, it is false that there are confirmatory signs (Mark 16:20; Heb. 2:3-4) today. Those who argue that the miraculous gifts of the Holy Spirit are available today must affirm, by implication, that additional revelation is needed today (and thus, if this view is true, the Bible is insufficient with regard to the information man needs to know in order to be saved and remain saved). However, it is false that the Bible is insufficient with regard to providing man all of the information he needs to know that pertains to salvation (cf. John 16:13; 2 Tim. 3:16-17; 2 Pet. 1:3). Therefore, it is false that additional revelation is needed today, and thus is false that the miraculous gifts of the Holy Spirit are available today. Hendricksen has argued this in the following manner:

> In connection with such special gifts (i.e. the gifts which enabled one to perform the signs of Mark 16:17-19, C.P.)... B.B. Warfield states, "These gifts were part of the credentials of the apostles as the authoritative agents in founding the Church... They necessarily passed away with it." That with the passing away of the apostolic age these gifts ceased is also the testimony of Chrysostom and Augustine. It was also the view of Jonathan Edwards: "These extra gifts were given in order to the founding and establishing of the church in the world. But since the canon of scripture has been completed, and the church fully founded and established, these extraordinary gifts have ceased." Among others who expressed similar views are Matthew Henry, George Whitefield, Charles H. Spurgeon, Robert L. Dabney, Abraham Kuyper, Sr., and W.G.T. Shedd (690).

Confirmation By The Signs

The apostles, having gone forth, preaching everywhere "the Lord working with them, and confirming the word by the signs that followed." This final phrase in the text includes two present participles (i.e. ***sunergountos***–working, and ***bebaiountos***–confirming). Note there are two things attributed to the Lord (working with them and confirming the word). The former does not necessarily include the miraculous. However, the latter must. "Working with them" is from ***sunergountos***. The Lord was working with them through the miraculous, but He also worked with them through the non-miraculous (i.e. His general providential care and through prayer [cf. Matt. 28:20; Rom. 8:28; 2 Cor. 1:8-11; Philip. 1:12-13, 19, et al]). He does not work with us today through the miraculous, but surely He will work with, and in, us today, not separate and apart from the word, but in conjunction with the word. Paul wrote, "Therefore, my beloved, even as ye have always obeyed, not as in my presence only, but now much more in my absence, work out your own salvation with fear and trembling; for it is God who works in you both to will and to work, for His good pleasure" (Philip. 2:12-13).

In his comments on these two present participles, Lenski has written the following: "Note the durative force of ***sunergountos***, likewise of the next present participle ***bebaiountos***. Confirming the Word was done in addition to working with the disciples" (774). This Greek term (***bebaiountos***) which is translated with our English word, **confirming**, means "to prove its truth and divinity" (Thayer 99). Arndt and Gingrich say "the saving message was guaranteed to us" (138). Bagster says that here it means: "to strengthen or establish by arguments or proofs, ratify" (68). It was "the word" that the Lord was confirming. Having gone forth, this is the word they preached (verse 20). And the Lord was confirming this word by "the signs following upon it" (***epakoloutheo***–to follow after, close upon, Vine, Vol. 2 111). See 1 Tim. 5:10, 24; 1 Pet. 2:21 for additional usage of this term **follow** (***epakoloutheo***). "The signs did not merely follow, they acted as a kind of authenticating signature to the word" (Moulton and Milligan, 238). That the term here translated, **follow**, entails the idea of "authenticating" the word is cited by Arndt and Gingrich in evidence from The Tebtunis Papyri and the Elephantine Papyri (282).

In conclusion, we affirm that powerfully, and sufficiently, the Lord confirmed the word.

> *And a thing once confirmed is forever confirmed*! If the court proves a man innocent of a charge, does it have to convene and reaffirm the man's innocence every year? Certainly not! One merely has to check the written record.

> Does Moses have to come back and again call forth the plagues on Egypt for us to believe that they were done? Does Jesus have to come back and again perform miracles for us to believe that He is the Son of God? We now have the written record to make believers (John 20:30-31). If one cannot be convinced by the Bible, he would not be convinced if one should rise from the dead (Luke 16:19-31) (Hobbs 12).
>
> Therefore, we ought to give the more earnest heed to the things that were heard, lest haply we drift away from them. For if the word spoken through angels proved steadfast, and every transgression and disobedience received a just recompense of reward; how shall we escape, if we neglect so great a salvation? Which having at the first been spoken by the Lord, was confirmed unto us by them that heard; God also bearing witness with them, both by signs and wonders, and by manifold powers, and by gifts of the Holy Spirit, according to his own will (Heb. 2:1-4, ASV).

WORKS CITED

Arndt, William F. and Wilbur F. Gingrich. *A Greek-English Lexicon of The New Testament and Other Early Christian Literature*, 1957. Chicago: U of Chicago P, 1973.

Bagster, Samuel, *The Analytical Greek Lexicon.* London: Samuel Bagster And Sons, 1967.

Crampton, W. Gary. "A Call for Christian Rationality" *The Trinity Review.* 196 (2001) : 1-4.

Elkins, Garland. "A Review of the Highers-Bishop Debate". *The Spiritual Sword.* 12.3 (1981).

Hendricksen, William. *New Testament Commentary Exposition of the*

Gospel According to Mark. 1975. Grand Rapids: Baker Book House, 1990.

Hobbs, A. G. "The Purpose of Miracles has been Fulfilled" *The Spiritual Sword.* 5.3 (1974).

Hofius, O. *The New International Dictionary of New Testament Theology*, Gen. Ed. Colin Brown. Vol. 2. Grand Rapids: Zondervan, 1976. 3 vols.

Jamieson, Robert, A. R. Fausset, and David Brown. *A. Commentary Critical, Experimental, and Practical on the Old and New Testaments.* Vol. 6. Grand Rapids: Wm. B. Eerdmans, 1961. 6 vols.

Lenski, R. C. H., *The Interpretation of St. Mark's Gospel.* Minneapolis: Augsburg Publishing House, 1964

McGarvey, J. W. *The New Testament Commentary Matthew-Mark.* St. Louis: Christian Publishing Company, 1875.

Moulton, James Hope, and George Milligan. *The Vocabulary of the Greek New Testament.* 1930. Grand Rapids: William B. Eerdmans, 1976.

Rengstorf, K.H., *Theological Dictionary of the New Testament.* 1971. Vol. 7. Grand Rapids: Wm. B. Eerdmans, 1978. 10 vols.

Rienecker, Fritz. *A Linguistic Key to the Greek New Testament.* Grand Rapids: Zondervan, 1976.

Thayer, Joseph Henry. *Greek-English Lexicon of the New Testament.* 1962. Grand Rapids: Zondervan, 1973.

Vine, W. E. *Vine's Expository Dictionary of New Testament Words.* 1940. Olphants Ltd., 1952. 4 vols.

CHAPTER 6

JESUS: THE REVELATION OF THE FATHER

The title of this chapter and the text for study (John 14:6-11) serve as reminders of a fundamental scriptural implication, viz. the need for divine revelation. In order for man to (1) know that God exists, (2) know something about the nature of God, and (3) know his responsibility to God, he must have revelation from God. This is what Paul, in principle, affirmed when he wrote, "For what man knows the things of a man, except the spirit of the man which is in him? Even so no one knows the things of God" (1 Cor. 2:11). Jeremiah declared, "O Lord, I know that the way of man is not in himself; It is not in man that walks to direct his own steps" (Jer. 10:23).

Traditionally, it has been correctly affirmed that God has revealed Himself to man through two basic types of revelation: (1) General Revelation and (2) Special Revelation. General revelation consists of what God has revealed about Himself through (1) the physical universe, (2) the physical world, and (3) man himself. Such Bible passages as Psalm 19:1-6; 139:14; Acts 14:17; Rom. 1:20, et al, show the validity of general revelation. Through general revelation man can ***know*** (1) God exists, (2) something about God's nature (cf. Rom. 1:20), (3) he owes his origin to the creative power of God, and (4) he is responsible to God.

However, there are many things in reference to God which cannot be known from a study of general revelation, viz. specifics of the Godhead, what man must do to be saved and remain saved, the nature and results of sin, the nature of the church, and many other essential matters. Therefore, there exists the need for ***special*** revelation from God. The only source of this complete and final revelation from God we confidently affirm to be the Bible. (NOTE: Although it is not the purpose of this chapter to prove that the Bible is the inspired, inerrant, and authoritative word of God, the evidence which demands this conclusion must, and can, be set forth.)

Within the overall scope of special revelation is that area with which we are concerned in this chapter, viz. the Person and Work of Jesus Christ and how He (Jesus Christ) is the revelation of the Father. Specifically, in this chapter, the matter of attention is "Jesus: The Revelation Of The Father" in the Gospel of John and, in particular, in light of John 14:6-11.

The Relationship Of Jesus And The Father In The Gospel Of John

The Gospel of John is, in a special and unique way, the book that reveals the Father. In Matthew the Father is mentioned 44 times, in Mark 5 times, in Luke 17 times, and in John 122 times. Every chapter in John contributes in a beautiful way to the development of this theme as seen in the following:

1. In chapter one, Jesus, "the only begotten Son, who is in the bosom of the Father," has declared Him (the Father)" (John 1:18).
2. In chapter two, Jesus is the One who is consumed by zeal for the Father's house (John 2:17).
3. In chapter three, "The Father loves the Son, and has given all things into His hands" (John 3:35).
4. In chapter four, Jesus declares that "the true worshipers will worship the Father in spirit and truth: For the Father is seeking such to worship Him" (John 4:23).
5. In chapter five, Jesus claims "I do not seek My own will, but the will of the Father who sent Me" (John 5:30).

6. In chapter six, Jesus affirms "the living Father sent Me, and I live because of the Father" (John 6:57).
7. In chapter seven, He knows the Father for He says, "I am from Him, and He sent Me" (John 7:29).
8. In chapter eight, Jesus rebuked His opponents saying, "Ye know neither Me, nor My Father: If you had known Me, you would have known My Father also" (John 8:19).
9. In chapter nine, Jesus informed the blind man whom He had healed that he (the blind man) had, in seeing and talking with Jesus, both seen and talked with the Father's Son (John 9:35-37).
10. In chapter ten, Jesus claims that the Father both knows and loves Him (John 10:15, 17).
11. In chapter eleven, Jesus thanks the Father (John 11:41).
12. In chapter twelve Jesus speaks just as the Father has told Him (John 12:49-50).
13. In chapter thirteen, Jesus knew when His hour had come that He should depart from this world to the Father (John 13:1).
14. In chapter fourteen, Jesus is THE way to the Father (John 14:6), and he who has seen Jesus has seen the Father (John 14:9).
15. In chapter fifteen, he who hates Jesus hates the Father also (John 15:23).
16. In chapter sixteen, Jesus says, "All things that the Father has are Mine" and "I am not alone, because the Father is with Me" (John 16:15, 32).
17. In chapter seventeen, Jesus had glory with the Father before the world was, and now prays that His disciples be one as He and the Father are one (John 17:5, 21).
18. In chapter eighteen, Jesus has a cup to drink that His Father gave Him (John 18:11).
19. In chapter nineteen, all power or authority comes from above (John 19:11) from the Father (John 17:2).
20. In chapter twenty, Jesus promised to ascend to His Father (John 20:17).
21. In chapter twenty-one, the book is remarkably concluded with: "And there are also many other things that Jesus

did, which if they were written one by one, I suppose that even the world itself could not contain the books that would be written. Amen" (John 21:25).

In addition to the foregoing material in reference to the relationship of Jesus and the Father in the Gospel of John there are various other specific characteristics of the Father that Jesus reveals, and John records. In part, they are the fact that the Father seeks (John 4:23), the Father works (John 5:17), the Father raises the dead (John 5:21), the Father gives (John 6:31, 32, 37), the Father draws (John 6:44), the Father honors (John 8:54), the Father knows (John 10:15), and the Father sanctifies (John 10:36; 17:17). Truly the Gospel of John reveals the Father!

The Affirmation Of The Claim (John 14:6)

The text (John 14:6-11) can be sub-divided into three sections. They are (1) the ***affirmation*** of the claim, (2) the ***explanation*** of the claim, and (3) the ***verification*** of the claim. Each of these areas shall be considered in light of the overall theme: "Jesus: The Revelation Of The Father".

Verse six contains the affirmation of the claim. "Jesus said to him, 'I am the way, the truth, and the life: No one comes to the Father except through Me.'" Jesus made this claim in answer to Thomas' question, "Lord, we do not know where you are going; and how can we know the way?" (John 14:5). Although Jesus had informed the disciples that He was returning to the Father, they were slow to understand. Thomas said they knew not where He (Jesus) was going, and thus they did not know the way. Jesus then declared that He is the way to the Father, and He is the *only* way.

This statement (John 14:6) is one of the great "I am" statements of Jesus recorded in the Gospel of John. These statements are truly marvelous and unique in that each one of them reveals some important characteristic concerning the Person and Work of Jesus. Although there are other "I am" statements of Christ, those relevant to this study in the Gospel of John are as follows:

1. "I am the bread of life" (John 6:35).
2. "I am the light of the world" (John 8:12).
3. "Before Abraham was, I AM" (John 8:58).
4. "I am the door of the sheep" (John 10:7).
5. "I am the good shepherd" (John 10:11).
6. "I am the resurrection and the life" (John 11:25).
7. "I am the true vine" (John 15:1).
8. "I am the way, the truth, and the life" (John 14:6).

With the exception of number three, all of the above statements are figurative in nature. Each is an expression which teaches, in a figure, something about the Person and Work of the Christ. For example, Jesus said, "I am the door" (John 10:7). Now quite clearly it is the case that Jesus is not a *literal* door. However, He is *like* a door. A door is the means through which one is able to enter a house, a building, a room, etc. Through Christ, one is able to enter into the blessings and privileges of salvation. Through Christ, one enters the house of God which is the church (1 Tim. 3:15). One enters, through Christ, by submitting his will to the will of Christ (i.e. through obeying His word, Matt. 7:21).

"The Way"

"I am the way, the truth, and the life". Here, certain aspects of our Lord's Person and Work are presented through the use of three figures. First, Jesus stated that He is the way. Obviously, He is not a *literal* way upon which we travel. However, He is, in a figure, *the* way. He provides the pathway that man must travel spiritually in order to get from earth to heaven (Matt. 7:13-14). Through His blood, He provides **"a new and living way"** through which man is able to be reconciled to God (Heb. 10:19-20; cf. Eph. 2:16). ***The way of the cross leads home***. The Old Testament prophet Isaiah spoke of "a highway. . . And a road, and it shall be called The Highway of Holiness; the unclean shall not pass over it; But it shall be for others . . ." (Isa. 35:8). Jesus is the way of which the prophet spoke in that Jesus established that Way (the church). In the book of Acts the expression **"the Way"** is used repeatedly in reference to Christ, and those who follow His system. Saul of Tarsus persecuted those of this Way (Acts 9:2). Faithful gospel preachers were said to be servants of the Most High God Who proclaim "the way of salvation" (Acts 16:17). Some "did not believe but spoke evil of the Way" (Acts 19:9). There arose a great commotion about the Way (Acts 19:23). Paul confessed that before becoming a Christian he had "persecuted this Way to the death" (Acts 22:4). He persecuted Jesus Who claims to be the way (Acts 9:5; John 14:6). He persecuted Jesus in that he persecuted the church which belongs to Jesus (1 Cor. 15:9; Gal. 1:13). The church of Christ and the idea of the way are synonymous in the New Testament. Paul said, "But this I confess to you, that according to the Way which they call a sect, so I worship the God of my fathers, believing all things that are written in the Law and the Prophets" (Acts 24:14).

The way that we need to travel spiritually must be made known to us by divine revelation. The way of man is not in himself (Jer. 10:23). We have turned everyone to his own way (Isa. 53:6), but the way that seems right to a man has as its end the way of death (Prov. 14:12; 16:25). Therefore, Jesus came as the way — **living** the way, **showing** the way, **providing** the way, and **establishing** the way.

"The Truth"

Jesus not only claimed to be the way, but He said, "I am. . . the truth." Again, we believe this to be metaphorical language. He is the truth in that He speaks the truth and reveals the truth on those most crucial issues of life. He claimed, "For this cause was I born, and for this cause I have come into the world, that I should bear witness to the truth" (John 18:37). He brought grace and truth (John 1:17). His life is the epitome of complete love for, and loyalty to, the truth. Never once was He ashamed of it; never once did He compromise it. He was full of truth (John 1:14). He told the truth (John 8:45).

Truth is one of the frequently recurring words in the Gospel of John. Worship must be in truth (John 4:24). Man can know the truth and experience freedom through a knowledge of the truth (John 8:32). The Holy Spirit (the Spirit of Truth - John 14:17; 15:26) was promised to the apostles that they might be guided into all the truth

(John 16:13). Man is sanctified through the truth which is the Word of God (John 17:17).

"The Life"

Jesus not only claimed to be the way and the truth, but He said, "I am. . .the life." Here is an example of the figure of speech known as metonymy (the effect is put when the cause is meant). Life is what Jesus produces. He is the source of life. He came that we might have life and have it abundantly (John 10:10). In Him was life (John 1:14). To have life we must come to Him (John 5:40). He is the bread of God from heaven that gives spiritual life (John 6:33). Thus, He is the bread of life (John 6:48). He gave His flesh for the life of the world (John 6:51). Unless we eat of His flesh and drink of His blood, which is equivalent to hearing and obeying His words (John 6:63), we have no life (John 6:53). He is the resurrection and the life (John 11:25). Through His appearing, He has abolished death and "brought life and immortality to light through the gospel" (2 Tim. 1:10). He is the life, because His way of life provides the "promise of the life that now is, and of that which is to come" (1 Tim. 4:8). Christianity provides the greatest way to live now (in this life), and the greatest way to prepare for death and what lies beyond, with the promise of eternal life. Through a knowledge of Him, we have all things that pertain to life and godliness (2 Pet. 1:3).

THE WAY- **THE** TRUTH - **THE** LIFE. He is not merely **a** way, **a** truth, or **a** life. He is exclusively **THE** way, **THE** truth, and **THE** life. There is no other way of salvation (Acts 4:12). There is no other source of the truth that saves (cf. John 16:13; John 8:31-32). There is no other source of eternal life (1 John 5:12).

The Explanation Of The Claim (John 14:7-9)

In verses seven through nine, Jesus further explained what was set forth in the claims of verse six. He said:

> If you had known Me, you would have known My Father also: and from now on you know Him, and have seen Him.

> Philip said to Him, "Lord, show us the Father, and it is sufficient", for Jesus said to him, "Have I been with you so long, and yet you have not known Me, Philip? He who has seen Me has seen the Father; so how can you say, 'show us the Father'?" (John 14:7-9).

Jesus came into the world to declare (unfold) the Father (John 1:18). The word translated *declared* is ***exegeomai*** from which we get the word *exegete.* It means to "explain, interpret, tell, report, describe" (Arndt and Gingrich 275). If they had truly discerned the nature of Jesus they would also have discerned the nature of the Father. One cannot know the Father without knowing the Christ who reveals the Father (John 17:3). Thus, to see and know the Son is to see and know the Father. "He who has seen Me has seen the Father; so how can you say, 'show us the Father?'" (verse 9). This does not mean that to see Jesus was to see the Father literally. "No one has seen God at any time" (John 1:18). What is meant is that to see Jesus is to see the Father REPRESENTATIVELY. Christ is "the express image of His (the Father's) person" (Heb. 1:3). The word translated *"express image"* (Gk. ***character)*** means "the exact expression (the image) of any person or thing, marked likeness, precise reproduction in every aspect (cf. facsimile)" (Thayer 665). Arndt and Gingrich say the words means "an exact representation of His (God's) nature" (884). We sometimes say that a certain child is the very image of his or her parent. If you want to know what the parent looked like, just look at the child. However, such is not a perfect image. In many ways the child will not look, or act, like the parent. However, it is not so with Jesus. Jesus is the **exact** image of His Father. All that God is, in His nature and character, is expressed perfectly by the incarnate Son.

This perfect likeness between the Father and the Son is seen in Jesus' statement, "Do you not believe that I am in the Father, and the Father in Me?" (John 14:10). This emphasizes the unity of the Father and Son. They are one (John 10:30). However, they are one in NATURE not in PERSON. Jesus is in the Father in that the Father's will guides, directs, and motivates Him. Prophets were said to be "in the Spirit" when they said what the Spirit commanded and directed

(Matt. 22:43). The Father is in the Son in that all the fullness of the Godhead dwells bodily in Christ (Col. 2:9). Jesus was God manifested in the flesh (1 Tim. 3:16). The Father, therefore, is seen in the Son, for it pleased the Father that in Him should all fullness dwell (Col. 1:19).

The Verification Of The Claim (John 14:10-11)

In verses ten and eleven, Jesus set forth two lines of evidence that serve as sufficient evidence to warrant the conclusion that He is the revelation of the Father. He said, "The words that I speak to you I do not speak on My own authority: but the Father who dwells in Me, does the works. Believe Me that I am in the Father, and the Father in Me: or else believe Me for the sake of the works themselves" (John 14:10-11).

The first line of evidence to which our Lord appeals here as proof that He is the revelation of the Father is His words. He said, "The words that I speak to you I do not speak on My own authority. . ." (verse ten). The words of Jesus Christ are sufficient proof that He is more than a man. He is divine.

His words are spiritual (John 6:63). His words are authoritative (Luke 4:32). His words are astonishing (Mark 10:24). His words are simplistic (As an example of the marvelous simplicity of His words note how He illustrated His lessons, e.g. salt, light, leaven, soil, children, birds, flowers, etc.). His words are wise and profound (Matt. 13:54; Luke 4:22). His words are powerful (Matt. 8:16; Mark 4:38; Luke 4:36). His words are unanswerable (Matt. 22:47; Luke 14:6). His words are flawless (Luke 20:26). His words are faith-producing (John 4:41-42), life-giving (John 6:63, 68), and peace-bringing (John 16:33). His words are enduring and eternal (Matt. 24:35). Some of His enemies said "He has a demon, and is mad; why do you listen to Him?" (John 10:20). However, the honest will admit, "These are not the words of one who has a demon" (John 10:21). Truly, "No man ever spoke like this man!" (John 7:46). Jesus' words–His parables, His beatitudes, His debates, His prayers, His sermons, and His private conversations–serve as adequate evidence that He is THE revelation of the Father.

The second line of evidence to which our Lord appeals as proof of His claim to be the Son of God, and thus the revelation of the Father, is His works. He said, "The Father who dwells in Me, does the works. Believe Me that I am in the Father and the Father in Me: or else believe Me for the sake of the works themselves" (John 14:10-11). The implication here is that if one cannot accept the full import of Jesus' words, (wherein He claims to be in the Father and the Father in Him), he cannot deny the reality of Jesus' miracles or works. The works of Jesus are the ultimate proof that He is divine. The word translated *works* ***(ergon)*** refers to the "sundry signal acts of Christ, to rouse men to believe in Him and to accomplish their salvation" (Thayer 248; Arndt and Gingrich 307-308). His works demonstrate the divine attributes of omnipresence, omniscience, and omnipotence (John 1:48-49; 2:1-11; 2:24-25; 4:17-19). His works demonstrate His power over nature (John 2:1-11), disease (John 5:1-9), material things (John 6:5-14), the devil (John 12:31-33), and death (John 11:41-46; 20:1-29). Truly, because "such mighty works are performed by His hands" (Mark 6:2), we must conclude, even as He affirmed, that the same works bear witness that the Father has sent Him (John 5:36). Both the words and the works of Jesus constitute sufficient evidence that He is "The Revelation of the Father".

The Sufficiency Of The Revelation (John 14:8)

In verse eight of the text is a significant statement made by Philip and recorded by the Holy Spirit. "Philip said to Him, 'Lord, show us the Father and it is sufficient for us" (John 14:8). Philip said if Jesus would show them the Father it would be enough. The idea behind the word *sufficient* is that of being satisfied and contented with what has been shown. The revelation of the Father is sufficient. Jesus' revelation of the Father is that which is sufficient and concerning which we can say, "It is enough. Nothing more is needed." Jesus' revelation of the Father is sufficient because:

1. There can be no greater revelation of God than that in a person, viz. when that Person is the Only Son of God.
2. Of none other than the Son and the Holy Spirit, could it

be said that the Father is, in every way like that One, without degrading God.

3. There can be no higher aspiration of man than to know God. It is higher than the aspiration to climb to the top of the corporate ladder, higher than aspiring to the Presidency of the United States, and higher than aspiring to walk on the moon.
4. *Everything* we need to know about God has been revealed by Jesus.
5. Jesus, as the revelation of the Father, is worthy of the worship of all creatures (Col. 1:18; Heb. 1:6). Since only God is worthy of worship (Rev. 22:9), and Jesus is to be worshipped (Philip. 2:10; Heb. 1:6), then Jesus is the perfect, the final, complete, and sufficient revelation of God.

Conclusion

Jesus came from heaven to earth that we might be able to go from earth to heaven. He traveled the road from heaven to Calvary that we might travel from Calvary to heaven. He came and demonstrated to man what God is that man might be more what he ought to be.

> God, who at various times and in various ways spoke in time past to the Fathers by the prophets, has in these last days spoken to us by His Son, Whom He has appointed heir of all things, through Whom also He made The worlds; Who being the brightness of His glory and the express image of His person, and upholding all things by the word of His power, when He had by Himself purged our sins, sat down at the right hand of the Majesty On High (Heb. 1:1-3).

> As His divine power has given to us all things that pertain to life and godliness, through the knowledge of Him who called us by glory and virtue, by which have been given to us exceedingly great and precious promises, that through

these you may be partakers of the divine nature, having escaped the corruption that is in the world through lust (2 Pet. 1:3-4).

WORKS CITED

Arndt, William F. and Wilbur F. Gingrich. *A Greek-English Lexicon of The New Testament and Other Christian Literature.* 1957. Chicago: U of Chicago P, 1973.

Thayer, Joseph Henry. *Greek-English Lexicon of The New Testament.* 1962. Grand Rapids: Zondervan, 1973.

CHAPTER 7

STEPHEN'S DEFENSE

Primarily, only the events of one day in the life of Stephen are recorded in the Sacred Writings. However, from that one day, sacred history records one of the greatest defenses of the Christian faith ever made. This defense, with the circumstances surrounding it, is recorded in Acts 6:8-7:60. Herein is one of the greatest sermons ever preached that is powerful in its presentation, logical in its lessons, and dynamic in its defense of the gospel of Jesus Christ. The recorded words of Stephen, and the events and circumstances surrounding these words, can be considered in light of (1) the ***debate***, (2) the ***defense***, and (3) the ***disposition*** of Stephen.

The Debate

Luke wrote, "Then there arose some from what is called the Synagogue of the Freedmen (Cyrenians, Alexandrians, and those from Cilicia and Asia), disputing with Stephen" (Acts 6:9). There was ***disputation***. The force of the Greek text is that they kept on disputing. Stephen was continuously debating these Jews. Observe that there were several with whom Stephen was debating. Much like Paul, when he arrived at Athens (Acts 17:17-18), Stephen was willing to meet as many as necessary as he was set for "the defense of the gospel" (Philip. 1:17).

Could it be that one of those whom Stephen engaged in debate was the young man Saul who, himself, years later, would become one of the great defenders of the Christian faith? Some of those with whom Stephen was debating were from Cilicia (Acts 6:9). Saul was from Cilicia (Acts 22:3), and he was present when Stephen was attacked and stoned to death (Acts 7:58; 22:20).

Some think it is unchristian to debate. I remember a preacher once saying, "I am going to leave the debating to someone else . . . We don't need to defend the faith as we need to enjoy the faith." If someone could have convinced Stephen of such, he could have saved his life. Those who speak disparagingly of all disputation and debate imply that Stephen died in vain. However, truly great gospel preachers have seen the value of *honorable* public discussion and debate. Following his first debate in 1820, Alexander Campbell wrote the following:

> We ardently wish for - we court discussion. Great is the truth and mighty above all things, and shall prevail. We constantly pray for its progress and desire to be valiant for it. Truth is our riches. Blessed are they that possess it in their hearts, who know its value, who feel its power, who live under its influence. They shall lie down in the dust in peace, they shall rest from their labors in hope, and in the morning of the resurrection they shall rise in glory and be recompensed for all their trials and sufferings in its support. (Richardson 30).

There was also ***misrepresentation***. The text says, "Then they secretly induced men to say, 'We have heard him speak blasphemous words against Moses and God'" (Acts 7:11). It is not uncommon for some, when they realize they cannot refute the truth of New Testament Christianity, to resort to a misrepresentation of those who are affirming and defending the truth. Observe from the account in the Acts of the Apostles that when "they were not able to resist the wisdom and the Spirit by which he (i.e. Stephen) spoke", THEN they began to do things which resulted in a misrepresentation of the truth and of Stephen who was defending the truth.

Stephen did not retaliate with personal attacks when he was misrepresented. Great debaters who possess the spirit of Christ, the greatest debater ever, are like a lamb when they are attacked personally, but like a lion when the truth (i.e. the doctrine) is attacked (cf. 1 Pet. 2:21-23; Matt. 15:3-14; 22:23-46; 23:1-39, et al).

The Defense

The presentation of Stephen was more apologetic, than homiletic, in nature. In fact, it is my conclusion that the preaching of the apostles of Christ and other first century evangelists was primarily apologetic in nature. Peter's Pentecost sermon (Acts 2:14-36) was a defense of the deity of Jesus. Paul's sermon at Athens (Acts 17:22-29) was a defense of the existence of the one, true God as well as a defense of Jesus' authority as proved by His historical resurrection from the dead (Acts 17:30-31).

Stephen's ***apologia*** was not merely a recitation of Old Testament history, but a dynamic defense of the divine plan of redemption fulfilled in Jesus Christ. The presentation by Stephen consisted of (1) powerful scriptural exposition and (2) powerful personal application. When questioned about the charges against him (Acts 6:13-14; 7:1), Stephen answered without one word of personal defense, but, with a marvelous familiarity with the Bible, he gave a powerful, pertinent review of Old Testament history (Acts 7:2-50). His apologetic discourse masterfully portrays the true nature of God and the divine purpose of the law of Moses. Beginning with the Abrahamic promise (Acts 7:2-8), Stephen then showed how God providentially worked in the lives of Abraham's son of promise, Isaac, and the twelve patriarchs, the sons of Jacob, especially Joseph (Acts 7:9-16). He reviewed the history of Israel, the nation in bondage (Acts 7:17-36), and Moses, the deliverer of the nation (Acts 7:37-43). Then from the tabernacle (Acts 7:44-45), to the temple (Acts 7:46-47), to the universe (Acts 7:48-50), Stephen declared the true nature of the infinite God. He then connected all of this scriptural exposition with a personal application to his disputants whom he claimed had, along with their fathers, rejected the Messianic plan and purpose of the law and the prophets. As their fathers had resisted the Holy Spirit by rejecting the prophets whose message He inspired, so those with whom Stephen was engaged in debate had resisted the Holy Spirit by rejecting the Just One (Jesus Christ) Whose coming was foretold in the law and the prophets (Acts 7:51-53).

The Disposition

Stephen is one of the greatest examples (other than the Lord, Himself) of how to defend the gospel of Christ against its adversaries. Peter wrote, "But sanctify the Lord God in your hearts, and always be ready to give a defense to everyone who asks you a reason for the hope that is in you, with meekness and fear" (1 Pet. 3:15). Stephen manifested the proper application of what Peter commanded to be done and how to do it.

Stephen spoke ***rationally***. The law of rationality says that one ought to justify his conclusions with adequate evidence. Stephen's defense was a presentation of the evidence that warranted his conclusions.

Stephen spoke ***wisely***. "They were not able to resist the wisdom . . . by which he spoke" (Acts 6:10). Stephen's defense is a fulfillment of what the Lord enjoined when He said, "Behold, I send you out as sheep in the midst of wolves. Therefore be wise as serpents and harmless as doves" (Matt. 10:16).

Stephen spoke ***spiritually***. "They were not able to resist . . . the Spirit by which he spoke" (Acts. 6:10). The Spirit by which Stephen spoke was the Holy Spirit. He spoke as the Spirit gave him utterance (cf. Matt. 10:17-20). It is my conclusion that Stephen spoke by the inspiration (cf. 2 Tim. 3:16) of the Holy Spirit (1 Cor. 2:13). No one living today has that measure of the Holy Spirit, which would enable him to speak by inspiration. However, anyone living today who would preach the gospel, and defend it properly, must speak the words of the Scriptures that were given by inspiration (2 Tim. 3:16-17; 1 Pet. 4:11).

Stephen spoke ***courageously***. He spoke in the face of death. Stephen dared to die for what he believed. He possessed remarkable courage.

Stephen spoke ***pointedly***. He said, "You stiff-necked and uncircumcised in heart and ears! You always resist the Holy Spirit;

as your fathers did, so do you" (Acts 7:51). The response to such plain and pointed language was ". . . they were cut to the heart, and they gnashed at him with their teeth" (Acts 7:54; cf. Acts 2:37).

Stephen spoke ***lovingly.*** There was no chip on his shoulder, or animosity in his heart (cf. Acts 7:57-60). Every indication is that Stephen spoke with a genuine love and concern for his hearers. They were wrong, and he was sorry that they were. It has been said that we need to condemn sin with a lump in the throat and a tear in the eye (cf. Jer. 9:1; Luke 19:41). A proper defense of the Christian faith does not entail any element of a mean or unkind spirit.

In my judgment, there was no greater Christian apologist during the twentieth century than Thomas B. Warren, Ph.D. (Vanderbilt University). I have tried to seriously study apologetics for the past thirty years and, during this time, I have not read, or heard, anyone whom I thought was more able to defend the Christian faith than Warren. He was an extremely gifted thinker, and yet his intellectual abilities did not exceed the loving concern and kindness he manifested toward his fellow disputants. As an example of this, at the conclusion of his historic 1978 debate on the existence of God with Dr. Wallace I. Matson (University of California at Berkeley), I heard Warren make one of the kindest, most loving appeals on behalf of Christianity, which I have heard (or read). Before thousands in attendance, he (Warren) addressed Dr. Matson and said:

> . . . I assure you, Dr. Matson, that. . . I try to preach that *every* man ought to love *every* other man on this earth; that if there is any answer to the racism we find in the world, it is in the religion of Jesus Christ; that the gospel has the great purpose of drawing all men into *one body*, that we may *all* be *one* in Christ, no matter whether you are from Africa, Europe, China, South America, or wherever. Paul makes this clear in Ephesians 2:13-16. And to intimate that we Christians do not love those who live in adultery or in homosexuality or that we do not love those who are even guilty of murder is to simply and flagrantly misrepresent us. The fact that we point out that these things are *sin* and that those who life in *willful disobedience* and who die in that condition will be *lost,* does *not* mean that we do not love them!

It was the same Lord who said to the woman taken in adultery, "Go thy way and *sin no more*," who said in Matthew 7:14,15, "Enter ye in at the narrow gate, for wide is the gate and broad is the way that leadeth unto destruction and many are there that enter in thereby. But narrow is the gate and strait the way that leadeth unto life and few there be that find it."

. . .And the Lord Jesus Christ who loved every person, even Wallace Matson, who was aware of his unhappy childhood, is aware of his problems even today, who loves him in spite of all that he has said against Him and who would forgive him — even as he would have forgiven *Judas*, if Judas had come to Jesus in penitence and, in effect, fallen down and said, "O Lord forgive me, I know I have been wrong." Our Lord would have been as willing to put His arm around Judas, in loving kindness and forgiveness, as He did around Peter. Peter *denied* Him; Judas *betrayed* Him. But Peter *repented!* And whose sermon do we have recorded in the second chapter of Acts but that of *Peter?* Dr. Matson, *that's* Christianity!

We are brought together in one body, to love each other, because we love Christ. . . There is no way that two people can come nearer to *Christ* without coming nearer to *each other!* How deeply sorry I feel for every person who has rejected God, for every person who has rejected the gift of God, for every person who in spite of the fact that Jesus said "Come unto me all ye that labor and are heavy laden and I will give you rest. Take my yoke upon you and learn of me, for I am meek and lowly in heart and ye shall find rest unto your souls."

I have had a great deal of tragedy happen in my life, but I'm not here to tell you about *me*, but about *Him who died for you*, that you might live forever (343-345).

Stephen spoke ***steadfastly***. The text says, "But he being full of the Holy Spirit, looked up steadfastly into heaven, and saw the glory of God, and Jesus standing on the right hand of God" (Acts 7:55, ASV). He remained focused. He was undaunted and unintimidated.

Stephen spoke ***prayerfully***. "And they stoned Stephen as he was calling on God and saying, 'Lord Jesus, receive my spirit.' Then he knelt down and cried out with a loud voice, 'Lord, do not charge them with this sin'" (Acts 7:59-60). We must defend the Christian faith, but it must be defended with prayer for ourselves, and for those before whom we make our defense.

Conclusion

Stephen's life on earth ended in a blaze of glory. Luke wrote:

> But he, being full of the Holy Spirit, gazed into heaven and saw the glory of God, and Jesus standing at the right hand of God, and said, "Look! I see the heavens opened and the Son of Man standing at the right hand of God!" Then they cried out with a loud voice, stopped their ears, and ran at him with one accord; and they cast him out of the city and stoned him. And the witnesses laid down their clothes at the feet of a young man named Saul. And they stoned Stephen as he was calling on God and saying, "Lord Jesus, receive my spirit." Then he knelt down and cried out with a loud voice, "Lord, do not charge them with this sin." And, when he had said this, he fell asleep (Acts 7:55-60).

The impact of Stephen's defense and death is seen in the words of one who, himself, became a great defender of the Christian faith. His name was Paul. He said, "When the blood of. . . Stephen was shed, I also was standing by consenting to his death, and guarding the clothes of those who were killing him" (Acts 22:20). Paul never forgot Stephen's defense. Stephen's martyrdom must have been a powerful motivating force in the memory of Paul. Stephen sealed his faith with his blood. Eventually, Paul did the same (cf. 2 Tim. 4:6-8).

Works Cited:

Richardson, Robert. *Memoirs of Alexander Campbell*. Philadelphia: J. B. Lippincott & Co., 1870.

Warren, Thomas B. and Wallace I. Matson. *The Warren-Matson Debate on the Existence of God.* Jonesboro: National Christian Press, 1978.

CHAPTER 8

THE DANGERS OF EVOLUTION

The term *evolution* comes from the Latin term ***evolvere*** which simply means to unfold or change (Webster 397). We may legitimately use the word evolution to refer to various changes that do not cross what biologists refer to as "phylogenetic boundaries" (Thompson 73). For example, there are changes that are associated with a caterpillar becoming a butterfly or buds developing into flowers. There are even changes which result in the development of new breeds of horses, cattle, or dogs. However, these are changes *within* groups (microevolution) and not changes *between* groups (macroevolution, 73). It is the latter of these two with which I am concerned in this chapter. This theory of General Evolution, or organic evolution, holds that all forms of life have come about through gradual, progressive changes in lower life forms. According to the evolutionary theory of origins, man has not been created by a Supernatural Power (God) but has evolved originally from non-living, non-intelligent, non-purposive forces of nature (i.e. from non-living, non-human things).

The Basic Danger of Evolution

There are numerous dangers of evolution. All of these dangers are the result of one basic, fundamental danger of evolution, viz. it is anti-God and promotes the philosophical view of life without God. Evolution is a completely naturalistic process. Evolution and creation cannot be harmonized. There is no middle ground. Thomas Huxley stated, "It is clear that the doctrine of evolution is directly antagonistic to that of Creation" (Coppedge 177). Clark and Bales stated, "There are others who could be quoted, but these quotations illustrate that as in the days of Darwin, so it is now that men often accept evolution because the only alternative is creation by God" (94).

At the heart of this basic danger of evolution (i.e. its anti-God nature) is the fact that evolution is utterly incompatible with the Genesis account of creation. This being the case, evolution is anti-biblical. He who attempts to harmonize evolution and the biblical account of creation is destined to compromise. Camp explained:

> Without considering all the disharmonies, we point to one outstanding one, the creation of Eve (Genesis 2:21). . . There is no figure of speech known which this could be that would make it true and harmonious with evolution, theistic or non-theistic. Though an analogy is a perfectly legitimate figure of speech, this cannot be an analogy of what actually occurred. An analogy is an extended likeness drawn and there is no likeness at all between the concept that the first woman was the natural child of non-human beings and the Genesis account of the formation of the first woman from the body of the first man (208-209).

Three Consequent Dangers

Given the anti-God nature of evolution, there are three attendant dangers that spring forth from this philosophical view of origins, which promote life without God. Evolution's negation of God results in a negation of (1) ***character,*** (2) ***conduct,*** and (3) ***compassion***. Carefully observe these dangers as they are implied in the following biblical passage:

> The fool has said in his heart, "There is no God." They are corrupt; They have done abominable works; There is none

> who does good. The Lord looks down from heaven upon the children of men to see if there are any who understand, who seek God. They have all turned aside; They have together become corrupt; There is none who does good, no not one. Have all the workers of iniquity no knowledge, who eat up my people as they eat bread, and do not call on the Lord? (Psalm 14:1-4).

Negation of Character

The text says, "The fool has said in his heart, 'There is no God.' They are corrupt; They have done abominable works" (Psalm 14:1). Note the connection between the affirmation of "no God" and a character that is corrupt. If there is no God–if man is not the result of the Creator and everything springs ultimately from natural causes–then there is no objective basis for the development of character. In fact, *character* would be a meaningless term. If evolution is true, everything is meaningless. If human beings are the result of some cosmic accident, blind non-purposive forces, then life is devoid of any true purpose or meaning.

Professor George Romanes was a bright young scientist who lived during the nineteenth century. He was a personal friend and colleague of Charles Darwin, and a professor at Oxford University. Romanes, as a young professor, lost his faith in God because of the influence of Darwin's evolutionary theories. However, the young professor regained his faith in the Creator and, prior to his death in 1894, he wrote:

> The negative evidence is furnished by the nature of man without God. . . I know from experience the intellectual distractions of scientific research, philosophical speculation, and artistic pleasures; but am also well aware that even when all are taken together and well sweetened to taste, in respect of consequent reputation, means and social position, &c., the whole concoction is but as high confectionery to a starving man. He may cheat himself for a time–especially if he is a strong man–into the belief that he is nourishing himself

> by denying his natural appetite; but soon finds he was made for some altogether different kind of food, even though of much less tastefulness as far as the palate is concerned . . . . There is no finality to rest in, while disease and death are always standing in the background. Custom may even blind men to their own misery, so far as not to make them realize what is wanting; yet the want is there. I take it then as unquestionably true that this whole negative side of the subject proves a vacuum in the soul of man which nothing can fill save faith in God (150-152).

Evolution rips the heart out of character in life, religion, education, and every worthwhile human endeavor. It is significant to note an observation of *U.S. News and World Report* with regard to the curriculum of colleges in the United States. Under the heading of "The New Trivial Pursuit" John Leo wrote:

> Until recently, it wasn't really essential to look deeply at curriculum. The components of a basic college education were well known and agreed upon. Now they aren't. Colleges are unsure of their mission. . . As a result of this confusion and drift, campuses are increasingly at the mercy of fads and trends. . . The University of Wisconsin has one (i.e. a course) on soap operas, and Purdue offers one called "The Biology of ER." Other current or recent courses include "Issues in Rock Music and Rock Culture" (Columbia University). . . Another hot subject is "porn studies." At colleges great and small, students now read pornography and watch porn movies for credit. "The pedagogic enshrinement of porn is by now an established fact," literary critic James Atlas noted in the *New Yorker* magazine. Students listen to lectures from porn stars, write porn fiction, film their own sex scenes, and take part in little inhibition-lowering classroom dramas, like donning S and M outfits and having themselves tied up and lightly whipped." "Some may see the vogue for porn on campus as a symbol of moral decay," wrote *Detroit News* columnist Cathy Young, "but maybe it says even more about our culture's intellectual

> decline." . . . The junk courses creep in because much of the professorate now believes that nothing can truly be known so nothing truly matters (20).

Is it not ironic that, twelve pages later in the same issue of *U.S. News and World Report*, there is an article on a controversial ruling of the Kansas State Board Of Education to prohibit statewide tests from mentioning evolution? Critics say this will mean "teachers will be less likely to teach evolution. . . and more vulnerable to community pressure to pooh-pooh Darwin's 140-year-old *The Origin of Species*" (Marcus 32). The connection between the fierce teaching of evolution in the educational institutions of America (Primary, Secondary, and Higher) for many years, and the observation that "much of the professorate now believe that nothing can truly be known, so nothing truly matters," is definite and real. The social, moral, and intellectual climate on most major college campuses today is the logical consequence of believing that there is no God and that man is simply the latest in a long chain of animals.

Negation of Conduct

Closely linked to the preceding point (i.e. evolution is dangerous because it negates the character of man with regard to meaningful endeavor) is the fact that evolution has a negative effect on moral conduct. Observe the connection between the negations of God (i.e. atheism, evolution), and immoral conduct, as described by the Psalmist. He stated, "The Lord looks down from heaven upon the children of men to see if there are any who understand, who seek God. They have all turned aside. They have together become corrupt; There is none who does good, no not one" (Psalm 14:2-3). Unbelief has no ultimate, objective standard of moral/ethical truth and thus everything is permitted. "There is none who does good, no not one" is the result of not retaining God in one's knowledge (Rom. 1:28). This being the case, no one can ever logically suggest that someone else's conduct is wrong, or that a person "ought" or "ought not" do thus and so. French existential philosopher, Jean Paul Sartre stated:

> The existentialist, on the contrary, finds it extremely embarrassing that God does not exist, for there disappears with Him all possibility of finding values in an intelligible heaven. There can no longer be any good *a priori*, since there is no infinite and perfect consciousness to think it. It is nowhere written that "the good" exists, that one must be honest or must not lie, since we are not upon the plane where there are only men. Dostoevsky once wrote, "If God did not exist, everything would be permitted"; and that, for existentialism, is the starting point. Everything is indeed permitted if God does not exist, and man is in consequence forlorn, for he cannot find anything to depend upon either within or outside himself. He discovers forthwith, that he is without excuse. . . Nor, on the other hand, if God does not exist, are we provided with any values or commands that could legitimize our behavior (485).

Evolution must acknowledge if man does not owe his origin to creation, then value is nothing more than a function of the human mind. If value is nothing more than a function of the human mind, then no conduct is better than any other. Herein is a grave danger of evolution, viz. the negation of values having any objectivity. What are the practical results of such a philosophical viewpoint? Richard Dawkins, a well known British evolutionist who has described himself as "a fairly militant atheist, with a fair degree of hostility toward religion" (qtd. in Thompson 74) has acknowledged:

> I am not advocating a morality based on evolution. I am saying how things have evolved. I am not saying how we humans morally ought to behave. . . My own feeling is that a human society based simply on the genes law of universal ruthless selfishness would be a very nasty society in which to live. But unfortunately, however much we may deplore something, it does not stop it being true (3).

"A very nasty society in which to live." Think about it! Dawkins is accurate in his conclusion. A society based simply on a philosophical viewpoint, which negates God, will be **"a very nasty society,"** because it has no objective reference point for ethics and morality. Any, and all, conduct, no matter how reprehensible, could logically be defended because, without God, it is impossible to argue for any objectivity with regard to "right" and "wrong". "Right" and "wrong" conduct is meaningless terminology without God. The only way there can be any objectivity to so-called "right and wrong conduct" is for there to exist some objective point of reference (God) Who is infinite in goodness and holiness, and thus, He correctly identifies what is really right and wrong conduct.

Negation of Compassion

The Psalmist further described the situation without God when he stated ". . .all the workers of iniquity (have) no knowledge who eat up my people as they eat bread" (Psalm 14:4). Here is disrespect for human life. But, again, it is the logical consequence of evolution. According to evolution, man may be more knowledgeable and more intellectual than the other animals, but he is still just an animal. And, like any animal, any human being is expendable. Herein lies another serious danger of evolution. It is a philosophical view that manifests little respect for the value of human life. According to evolution, everything works according to "the survival of the fittest." The weaker members of society are unfit and, according to the laws of nature, will not normally survive (cf. Darwin 323). Therefore, nature selects against the weaker animals and this is also the case for man, because he too is merely an animal. Carried to the logical consequence, if evolution is the true explanation of the origin of man, then why should any human being expect things to be different for him than for any animal? Weak horses are shot and put out of their misery, so why not weak human beings whether it be the fetus in the womb, the aged in the nursing home, or the retarded in the asylum? If evolution is true, then abortion, euthanasia, or any other kind of murder is not wrong. As Dylan Klebold and Eric Harris roamed Columbine High School, they approached seventeen year old Cassie Bernall. She was asked by one of the gunmen if she believed in God. She said yes. She was then asked why and ". . .they just blew her away" (Bernall 13). Someone had convinced those two young men that God does not exist, and their actions are the horrifying, but logical, consequences of life without God. If evolution (atheism) is true, then there is no difference between killing a cockroach or a human being.

Conclusion

The basic danger of evolution is seen in the fact that it is anti-God and thus promotes a philosophy of life without God. When man refuses to allow the evidence to convince him that God exists, and that the only rational explanation of the origin of the world and man is the creative power of God, then the next step is the *negation* of (1) ***character*** (2) ***conduct*** and (3) ***compassion***. When man does not "see fit to acknowledge God" (Rom. 1:28, NASV) in his thinking, then his life will be devoid of character and meaning, filled with immoral and unethical conduct, and robbed of compassion for other human beings (cf. Rom. 1:18-32).

Ultimately, there is the greatest danger of any false philosophy, viz. the danger of losing one's soul eternally. Evolution causes people to be lost, because it produces unbelief "and without faith it is impossible to please God, because anyone who comes to Him must believe that He exists and that He rewards those who earnestly seek Him" (Heb. 11:6, NASV). Herein is the most far-reaching danger of this anti-God philosophy called evolution which will tragically, and ultimately, be realized, ". . . when the Lord Jesus is revealed from heaven with His mighty angels, in flaming fire taking vengeance on those who do not know God" (2 Thess. 1:7-8). May good, right thinking people everywhere accept the challenge to meet head-on this dangerous false philosophy of evolution with the adequate evidence, which refutes evolution, and proves that, "In the beginning God created. . ." (Gen. 1:1).

Works Cited:

Bernall, Misty. *She Said Yes*. Farmington: Plough Publishing, 1999.

Camp, Robert A. "Theistic Evolution." *A Critical Look at Evolution.* Atlanta: Religion, Science, and Communication Research and Development Corporation, 1972.

Clark, Robert T. and James D. Bales. *Why Scientists Accept Evolution.* 1966. Grand Rapids: Baker Book House, 1976.

Coppedge *Evolution: Possible or Impossible*? Grand Rapids: Zondervan, 1975.

Dawkins, Richard. *The Selfish Gene.* New York: Oxford U P, 1976.

Darwin, Charles. "The Descent of Man." *Great Books of the Western World.* Ed. In Chief Robert Maynard Hitchius. Vol. 49. Chicago: Encyclopaedia Britannica, 1952. 54 vols.

Leo, John. "The New Trivial Pursuit". *U.S. News and World Report.* 127.8 (1999) : 20.

Marcus, David L. "Charles Darwin Gets Thrown Out of School" *U.S. News and World Report.* 127.8 (1999) 32.

Romanes, George John. *Thoughts on Religion.* 5th ed. London: Longmans, Green, and Co., 1895.

Sartre, Jean Paul. "Existentialism and Humanism." *French Philosophers from Descartes to Sartre.* Ed. Leonard M. Marsak. Cleveland: Meridian/World Publishing, 1961.

Thompson, Bert. "The Implications of Evolution." *Reason and Revelation.* 17 (1997) : 73-78.

Webster's New Collegiate Dictionary. Springfield: G&C Merriam, 1974.

CHAPTER 9

THE GREATNESS OF CHRISTIANITY

While in banishment at St. Helena, and conversing with General Bertrand who argued that Jesus of Nazareth was no more than a man, the exiled emperor Napoleon said, "I know men, and I tell you that Jesus Christ is not a man!. . . There is between Christianity and whatever other religions the distance of infinity" (Pierson 227-228). Napoleon's statement is a reminder of the greatness of Christianity. ***Greatness*** involves the characteristic of being markedly superior in character or quality. By ***Christianity***, I mean the religion of Jesus of Nazareth as revealed in the sixty-six books of the Bible. The Christian system was foreshadowed and prophesied in the Old Testament and was fully revealed in the New Testament writings. And so, when I speak of ***"the greatness of Christianity,"*** I mean the superior character and quality of the religion of Jesus Christ as set forth in the Bible.

The Greatness of Christ

Christianity is great because Jesus Christ is great. Christ, and His identity, provide the solid, unshakeable foundation of Christianity. He said that it was "on this rock" (i.e. His identity as "the Christ, the Son of the living God," Matt 16:16) that He would build His church (Matt. 16:18). When one becomes a Christian he believes Jesus really is who He claims (John 8:24), confesses this faith in Christ (Rom. 10:9-10) and, with a mind of repentance (Acts 2:38), is baptized into Christ for the remission of sins (Acts 2:38; 22:16; Rom. 6:3-4), seeks to do all things in the name of (i.e. by the authority of) Christ (Col. 3:17), and waits for this Jesus to return one day from heaven (1 Thess. 1:10). The Christian, though he has not seen Christ, loves Him (1 Pet. 1:8) and desires that Christ shall be magnified in his body (Philip. 1:20).

The greatness of Jesus Christ is attested to by the greatness of His life. It was an actual, historical life. He "was born of the seed of David according to the flesh" (Rom. 1:3). Peter affirmed the historical nature of Christ and Christianity when he wrote, "For we did not follow cunningly devised fables when we made known to you the power and coming of our Lord Jesus Christ, but were eyewitnesses of His majesty" (2 Pet. 1:16). His life was a unique life. Of no other person in human history, other than Jesus, can it be said, "He has done all things well" (Mark 7:37). No book was ever written on the deity of Muhammed, Joseph Smith, Mary Baker Eddy, et al. The greatness of Jesus is evidenced by the greatness of His words (John 7:46), His works (John 3:2), His influence (John 12:19), and His resurrection (Rom. 1:4).

Simon Greenleaf was Royall Professor of Law at Harvard University and succeeded Justice Joseph Story as Dane Professor of Law at Harvard in 1846. Greenleaf wrote a work entitled *A Treatise on the Law of Evidence* (1842). It is still considered a classic on evidence in the literature of legal procedure. He also wrote *An Examination of the Testimony of the Four Evangelists by the Rules of Evidence Administered in the Courts of Justice* (1847). Greenleaf gave tribute to Jesus Christ when he stated: "The character of Jesus exhibits no error, no sinister intention, no imprudence, no ignorance, no evil passion, no impatience, in a word, no fault; but all is perfect uprightness, innocence, wisdom, goodness and truth" (qtd. in Russell 66). Daniel Webster concurred with these sentiments when he said the following:

> The philosophical argument, especially that drawn from the vastness of the universe in comparison with the insignificance of the globe, has sometimes shaken my reason

> for the faith that is in me; but my heart has always assured me and reassured me that the gospel of Jesus Christ must be a divine reality. The Sermon on the Mount cannot be a human production. This belief enters into the very depths of my conscience, the whole history of man proves it (qtd. in Pierson 227).

In tribute to the greatness of Jesus Christ, A.T. Pierson cited Napoleon who said:

> You speak of Caesar, Alexander; of their conquests; of the enthusiasm they enkindled in the hearts of their soldiers; but can you conceive of a dead man, making conquests with an army faithful and entirely devoted to His memory? My army has forgotten me while living. Alexander, Caesar, Charlemagne and myself, have founded empires. But on what did we rest the creations of our genius? Upon force! Jesus Christ alone founded His empire upon love; and at this hour millions of men would die for Him. . . Now, that I am at St. Helena, alone, chained upon this rock, who fights and wins empires for me? What an abyss between my deep misery and the eternal reign of Christ, who is proclaimed, loved, adored, and whose reign is extending over all the earth! (231).

In reference to the greatness and superiority of Jesus Christ, Haygood has stated:

> The facts of His humanity and of His work and influence in the world forbid us to classify Jesus with men, and the recognition of His divinity alone explains the facts of His humanity. Considered as God-man all is in harmony; miracles take their proper place in the records of His history, and mind and nature, heaven and earth, God and man meet in Jesus, the Christ. But–if He be only a man–He is such a man as were a thousand times worth dying for and following forever, through time and eternity (60).

Christianity is great, and at the heart of this greatness of the religion of Jesus Christ is Christ Himself. Among the sons of men there has not risen greater than Jesus of Nazareth. He truly is:

> Christ Jesus. . . Literatures' loftiest ideal, philosophy's highest personality, criticism's supremest problem, theology's fundamental doctrine, spiritual religion's cardinal necessity–personally, socially, politically, economically, educationally, scientifically, nationally, internationally, the only hope of our head-dizzy, body-weary, soul-sick, heart-aching, sin-smitten, war-scarred world. Down from the heights of deity to the depths of humanity he came–to lift up, not cast down; to deliver, not doom; to bless, not curse; to save many, not destroy men. In life–misunderstood, misinterpreted, maliciously maligned, he was heaven's bread for earth's hunger; heaven's water for earth's thirst; heaven's light for earth's darkness; heaven's glory for earth's shame; heaven's grace for earth's guilt; heaven's peace for earth's strife; heaven's love for earth's hate; heaven's wealth for earth's poverty; heaven's clothing for earth's nakedness; heaven's salvation for earth's damnation; heaven's life for earth's death. . . History with Him left out is like astronomy with stars omitted, like botany with flowers forgotten, like geology with rocks thrown away. Though he had no stenographer and no pocketbook and owned no real estate, this Jesus is embedded in the world's history, regnant in the world's art, vocal in the world's music, eloquent in the world's literature, vital in the world's political areas and arenas.
>
> That Christ lives is testified to by historians with their Christ-pointing events, by chronologists with their Christ-honoring dates, by geographers with their Christ-blessed places, by architects with their Christ-honoring buildings, by painters with their Christ-praising pictures by sculptors with their Christ-glorifying statues, by poets with their Christ-loving verses. . . Of all examples of influence, Jesus is the most vivid and far-reaching. . . Many attacks have been made upon Jesus. He came unto His own and His own

> received Him not. Killing Him, they buried Him in a tomb hewn out of solid rock–and sealed it with a heavy stone, and set a guard there to watch. But the third day He arose from the grave and smashed at one blow Death's empire of skulls and skeletons–because, as Peter said, "it was impossible for Him to be holden of it. . . . Some say, "He was not divine"; but they cannot deny that He lived divinely. Some have tried to divest Him of His miraculous power, but He remains immortally the greatest of all miracles (Lee 76-77).

Intellectual Greatness

Christianity is great because of its intellectual greatness. It is the only religion that honors the law of rationality, which states that one ought to justify his conclusions by adequate evidence (Matt. 11:1-6; Luke 1:1-4; John 20:30-31; Acts 26:25; 1 Thess. 5:21; 1 Pet. 3:15; 2 Pet. 1:16-21; 1 John 4:1, et al). When Professor George Romanes, a young scientist of the nineteenth century, who was a student and friend of Charles Darwin, lost his faith in God, he struggled to regain that faith, which he did regain with even greater certainty. A few days before his death, at the young age of 46, he said, " I have now come to see that faith is intellectually justifiable. It is Christianity or nothing" (Romanes 349).

Moral Greatness

Christianity is great because of the moral greatness which characterizes it. The greatest kind of living is Christian living. Peter wrote, "Beloved, I beg you as sojourners and pilgrims, abstain from fleshly lusts which war against the soul, having your conduct honorable. . ." (1 Pet. 2:11-12). The word *honorable* (NKJV) in this text is translated from a Greek word which means "beautiful by reason of purity of heart and life. . . morally good, noble" (Thayer 322). An army chaplain was kneeling beside a wounded soldier on the battlefield. The chaplain asked the soldier if he wanted him to read something from the Bible. The soldier, near death, replied, "I'd rather have a drink of water. I'm thirsty." The chaplain gave the boy some water. Then the young soldier said, "I'm so cold." The chaplain took off his coat and wrapped it around the dying boy. The soldier looked at the chaplain and then said, "If there is something in that book that makes you do these things, please read it to me."

James Russell Lowell said:

> The worst kind of religion is no religion at all, and these men living in ease and luxury, indulging themselves in the amusement of going without religion, may be thankful that they live in lands where the gospel they neglect has tamed the beastliness and ferocity of the men who, but for Christianity, might long ago have eaten their carcasses like the South Sea Islanders, or cut off their heads and tanned their hides like the monsters of the French Revolution. When the microscopic search of skepticism, which had hunted the heavens and sounded the seas to disprove the existence of a Creator, has turned its attention to human society and has found a place on this planet ten miles square where a decent man can live in comfort and security, supporting and educating his children unspoiled and unpolluted; a place where age is reverenced, infancy respected, manhood respected, womanhood honored, and human life held in due regard–when skeptics can find such a place ten miles square on this globe, where the gospel of Christ has not gone and cleared the way and laid the foundation and made decency and security possible, it will then be in order for the skeptical literati to move thither and then ventilate their views. But so long as these men are dependent upon the religion which they discard for every privilege they enjoy, they may well hesitate a little before they seek to rob the Christian of his hope, and humanity of its faith, in that Savior who alone has given to man that hope of life eternal which makes life tolerable and society possible, and robs death of its terrors and the grave of its glooms (Smith 32).

Emotional Greatness

The religion of Jesus Christ possess emotional greatness. When understood and applied, Christianity provides the only way to truly and adequately deal with the suffering, adversity, and stress that is a part of life on earth (cf. John 16:33; Rom. 8:18; 2 Cor. 4:16-18; 1 Pet. 5:6-7). Christianity is concerned with good mental health (Philip. 4:6-7). Dr. James Fisher, an experienced psychiatrist, who had extensive experience of more than fifty years of practice in dealing with emotional, mental, and physical problems, once expressed the following observation about the emotional greatness of Christianity:

> I dreamed of writing a handbook that would be simple, practical, easy to understand, easy to follow. It would tell people how to live–what thoughts and attitudes and philosophies to cultivate, and what pitfalls to avoid in seeking mental health. I attended every symposium it was possible for me to attend and took notes on the wise words of my teachers and of my colleagues who were leaders in their field. And quite by accident I discovered that such a work had already been completed!
>
> If you were to take the sum total of all authoritative articles ever written by the most qualified of psychologists and psychiatrists on the subject of mental hygiene–if you were to combine them and refine them and cleave out the excess verbiage–if you were to take the whole of the meat and none of the parsley, and if you were to have these unadulterated bits of pure scientific knowledge concisely expressed by the most capable of living poets, you would have an awkward and incomplete summation of the Sermon on the Mount. And it would suffer immeasurably through comparison.
>
> For nearly two thousand years the Christian world has been holding in its hands the complete answer to its restless and fruitless yearnings. Here . . . rests the blueprint for successful human life with optimum mental health and contentment (Cramer 14-16).

Spiritual Greatness

Christianity is superior, in character and quality, to all other religions because of its spiritual greatness. It alone has the one true, efficacious plan which enables man to be in a right relationship with God. Only the gospel of Jesus Christ, and the plan of salvation revealed therein, are in harmony with (1) the infinite nature of God and (2) the sinful condition of man (cf. Rom. 3:23-28). In Jesus Christ, the infinite God is both just and justifier (Rom. 3:26). The Christian life is a forgiven life (1 John 1:7; Rev. 1:5). Furthermore, the spiritual greatness of Christianity provides the only rational way to prepare for death (cf. Psalm 116:15; Philip. 1:21; 2 Tim. 4:7-8; Rev. 14:13). Human experience, as well as biblical testimony, verify that to die as a Christian is the greatest way to die. No man who has faithfully lived the Christian life has ever denied it in death. However, many who have denied Christianity in life have attempted to renounce their infidelity in death.

Voltaire, the skeptic who boasted that with his single hand he would destroy the edifice of the Christian religion, which he said the twelve apostles built, died a horrible death. The nurse who was at his bedside, at his death, said, "For all the wealth in Europe I would not see another infidel die" (Lockyer 133). Russell eloquently contrasted the spiritual greatness of Christianity with some of those noted sentiments, which have denied the Christian faith. He wrote the following:

> A few years ago the most noted infidel in our country pronounced a funeral sermon by the graveside of his brother. These were his consoling words: "Life is a narrow vale between the cold and barren peaks of two eternities. We strive in vain to look beyond the heights. We cry aloud and the only answer is the echo of our wailing cry." Let Voltaire try what he can to do to offer condolence to any who have been hitherto disposed to trust the issues of life and death to the chances of unbelief. "Here is a flower for your casket: In man there is more wretchedness than in all animals put together. He loves life, and yet he knows that he must die. If he enjoys a transient good he suffers various evils, and is at last devoured by worms. I wish I had never been born."

> Contrast these rattling husks with the tender consolations of Christianity. "Let not your hearts be troubled. Ye believe in God believe also in Me. In My Father's house are many mansions. I go to prepare a place for you." Thus Christ flashes the light of His glorious pledge upon the darkness and its murky shadows flee away. "For me to live is Christ and to die is gain," says the inspired apostle (247-48).

Conclusion

In this chapter attention has been given to the greatness (i.e. the superior character and quality) of Christianity. Great is the Christian faith because of the greatness of Jesus Christ. Furthermore, the greatness of Christianity is manifested in its superior character and quality (1) ***intellectually***, (2) ***morally***, (3) ***emotionally***, and (4) ***spiritually***. Such greatness is evidence that (1) God exists, (2) the Bible is the Word of God, (3) Jesus is the Son of God, (4) Christianity is the one, true religion, and (5) all men everywhere ought to believe in, love, and obey Jesus Christ, and thus become, and remain, Christians. There is no religion in the same class as Christianity. H. W. Everest has shown the power of this argument when he wrote:

> Could man have produced it? Man can make his artificial lake, but could he have made the ocean, measured its waters, established its bounds, and correlated it with continents, winds, and suns? Man can erect the granite shaft, but could he have lifted the mountains to the sky and made them awful and sublime? So man could have written many things in the Bible and could have discovered many truths there revealed and sanctioned by the divine name, but could he have invented Christianity as a system? Are there not in it oceans whose waters he did not gather together, and mountains on whose summits he never stood? . . . Christianity purifies the heart and corrects the life. It destroys domestic and social tyranny. It elevates woman and secures the education of children. It undermines and destroys all social evils. It promotes science, and brings all nations into commercial harmony. It cares for the imbecile, the deaf and dumb, the

blind and the poor, as no other religion does. He who does not accept this statement is ignorant of the facts. It differs from all other systems in its fitness to become universal. It is founded on man's common religious nature. It meets the wants of all men, those which are deepest and most pressing. It has nothing in it partial and merely ethnic. It is suited to all ages and states of civilization, as well as to all zones. The missionary zeal and effort produced by Christianity are peculiar. It is propagated by the power of truth and love, not by the sword; by the self-sacrifice of its missionaries, and not by despotic power. It is flooding the world with Bibles, and sending the living heralds of the cross into all lands. What other religion can compare with it?. . . ***Christianity is the only religion that can endure in the light of reason and science, the only one that scientific and civilized man can accept and propagate. . . No other religion can produce one hundredth part of the evidence in its support. No other religion presents so clear, so full, and so faultless a revelation of God***. . . .Christianity is unlike all other religions in having a divine founder and savior. It is superior in that Christ is admitted to be superior to all other religious teachers. . . Christianity comes with a divine sanction. It brought life and immortality *to light.* It gives us not a mere hope and a theory concerning the life to come, but a grand *fact*. . . The statement is not true that Christianity is just like all other religions. . . Christianity is *superhuman*: its account of Creation; its unity; its prophecies; its sublime morality; its profound religious principles; its stupendous plan, comprehending time and eternity; its Jesus, a perfect man and a perfect manifestation of God, sinless, faultless, and divine; its triumph over the combined opposition of the Jewish nation and of the Roman Empire; the impossibility, on the supposition that Jesus was not what He claimed to be and hence in no sense the Author of Christianity, that any one of His disciples could have devised such a grand scheme and made it successful — all concur in demonstrating the supernatural character of this religion. There are no insuperable objections. The author of such a system must have been divine. . . What stronger evidence could be demanded? What stronger evidence is possible?" (201, 239-41, 358).

Works Cited:

Cramer, Raymond L. *The Psychology of Jesus and Mental Health.* 1959. Grand Rapids: Zondervan, 1974.

Everest, Harvey W. *The Divine Demonstration. A Text-Book of Christian Evidence*. 1884. Nashville: Gospel Advocate, 1972.

Haygood, Atticus G. *The Man of Galilee*. 1889. Marion: Cogdill, 1963.

Lee, R. G. *Grapes From Gospel Vines*. Nashville: Broadman Press, 1976.

Lockyer, Herbert. *Last Words of Saints and Sinners*. 1969. Grand Rapids: Kregel, 1975.

Pierson, Arthur T. *Many Infallible Proofs*. New York: Fleming H. Revell, 1886.

Romanes, E. *Life and Letters of George John Romanes* London: Longmans, Green, and Co., 1895.

Russell, Howard H. *A Lawyer's Examination of the Bible*. Chicago: Fleming H. Revell, 1893.

Smith, Wilbur M. *Therefore Stand.* 1945. Grand Rapids: Baker Book House, 1976.

Thayer, Joseph Henry. *Greek-English Lexicon of the New Testament*. 1962. Grand Rapids: Zondervan, 1973.

APPENDIX

THE BIBLE INVITES YOUR INVESTIGATION

The following noteworthy commendation was given the people of Berea by the historian, Luke: "These were more fair-minded than those in Thessalonica, in that they they received the word with all readiness, and searched the Scriptures daily to find out whether these things were so" (Acts 17:11). The religion of Jesus Christ has always invited honest examination and commended such when it occurs. And, when the fair-minded investigate thoroughly the claims of Christianity, the truth of the Christian faith becomes evident to them.

History records many examples of those who were either skeptical, or indifferent, to the claims of Jesus Christ but who, upon honest investigation of the New Testament, became believers. In an old work entitled, *The Young Man's Guide Against Infidelity*, and dated 1848, the author tells about one, Count Struenese, Prime Minister of Denmark in the latter eighteenth century, who endeavored to spread his philosophy of atheism and infidelity.

However, he studied Burnet's examination of the arguments for Christianity and ultimately the doubts were removed which had formerly occupied his mind. He stated the following:

> I never imagined that Christianity was founded upon such strong evidences. . . . After a calm examination, I have found them to be unexceptionable, and none, if they only take proper time. . .can ever examine them without being convinced of the truth. . . . The more I read, the more I grow convinced how unjust those objections are with which Christianity is charged (qtd. in Mitchell 390).

The invitation to investigate is still open. "'Present your case,' says the Lord. 'Bring forth your strong reasons…'" (Isa. 41:21). "'Come now and let us reason together', says the Lord'" (Isa. 1:18).

"REASONING" AGAINST REASON

Presently, there is in the church a movement, becoming more widespread, which de-emphasizes the importance of sound reasoning (logic) in coming to an understanding of what the Bible teaches. In some cases, this flight from reason by some of my dear brethren (all of whom I love and for whom I desire only the best) borders on *misology* (a hatred of reasoning).

Whenever you hear or read statements like "only *direct* statements tell us for certain what God thinks" or "no one has the right to bind something unless it is *explicitly* stated in Scripture," you can know that those making such statements do not understand the essential place of correct reasoning (deducing or inferring what the explicit statements of the Bible imply).

What is at stake here? Simply, the total relevancy and authority of the Bible. If we cannot correctly deduce or infer what the Bible implies, and if such deductions or inferences are not "bound," then the Bible does not have even one thing to say to you or me which we must, or must not, do. The only way you or I could ever know that we must do something the Bible teaches is by deducing (inferring) what the Bible states. This is the case, because nowhere does the Bible say even one thing to you or me *explicitly.* Just attempt to find (***without using deduction or inference***) *one* thing in the Bible which you *know* is addressed to you. It cannot be done. You cannot "**reason**" against reason!

THE RIGHT VIEW OF EDUCATION

When Daniel was captured and taken to Babylon (circa. 605-606 B.C.), he was in his youth (Dan. 1:3-4). Turner suggests that Daniel and his friends were teenagers at this time (11). The purpose of the Babylonian king was clear. He desired to thoroughly Chaldeanize, ethnically and religiously, these smart, good looking, talented youths. They would be educated in Babylonian language and literature, which would include learning Babylonian history, religion, law, politics, art, social customs, and cuisine (cf. Dan. 1:4ff). Concerted effort was made, not only to educate Daniel and his companions, but to influence them to deny their beliefs. Their names were changed. They were given new names, which obliterated the name of Jehovah God and gave honor to the Chaldean gods (cf. Dan. 1:6-7). Pfeiffer states:

> They knew from their Bibles the Genesis account of creation. Now they would be taught the story of how Marduk cut in two the monster Tiamat and made heaven and earth from the two parts of her body. They would learn about astrology and medicine, about Babylonian law and mathematics. Some of this would challenge beliefs that they had held from childhood. . . (206).

Although receiving instruction in the mysterious occult practices of the Babylonian religion, Daniel remained true to the One living God (cf. Dan. 2:28). From Daniel, Christian youth of today can learn the right view of education. Do not allow anyone, or anything, to rob you of your precious faith (1 Pet. 1:7). Keep the true and living God at the center of everything–even your education. There is one thing worse than a fool and that is an educated fool (cf. 2 Tim. 3:7). "The fear of the Lord is the beginning of knowledge" (Prov. 1:7).

RELIGIOUS DEBATE

During a Presidential Election year we often hear about political debate. The New Testament has much to say about religious debate. "Then there arose some. . . disputing with Stephen" (Acts 6:9). *Disputing* is in the present tense and means they "kept on disputing." They kept on debating.

Some think it is unchristian to debate. One preacher said, "... We don't need to defend the faith as much as we need to enjoy the faith." However, truly great gospel preachers have recognized the value of honorable public discussion and debate (cf. Acts 9:29; 17:16-17; Philip. 1:16-17, et al). As a student in the great classes on apologetics taught by the late Thomas B. Warren at Harding University Graduate School of Religion in Memphis, Tennessee, my attention was directed to the following marvelous statement from the pen of Alexander Campbell:

> If it were lawful, or if it were benevolent, to make a truce with error, then opposition to it would be both unjust and unkind... In proportion as a person is intelligent and benevolent, he will be controversial, if error exist around him. Hence, the Prince of Peace never sheathed the sword of the Spirit while He lived. He drew it on the banks of the Jordan and threw the scabbard away! (41).

Stephen followed His steps. May we do likewise (1 Pet. 2:21).

WAYS TO STRENGTHEN YOUR FAITH IN GOD WHILE LIVING IN A SKEPTICAL WORLD

Disbelief in God continues to grow at an alarming rate. According to the Associated Press, the number of American adults identifying themselves as atheists has more than doubled from 14.3 million in 1990 to 29.4 million in 2001 (Centerville 4). What can one do to strengthen faith in God, the Christ, and the Bible?

Study the Bible and learn what it actually teaches. Many who are skeptical in reference to the Bible have never carefully read the entire book. David Hume, a prince among skeptical philosophers, is reported to have remarked that he had never read the New Testament with attention.

Remember that the Bible encourages honest investigation. The crucifixion of intelligence is not a condition for entrance into the kingdom of God. Christianity does not fetter thought (cf. Acts 17:11; 1 Thess. 5:21).

Do not make a god of science. Science is valuable if used wisely. The pursuits of science are God-ordained (cf. Gen. 1:28). However, science has limitations. Science cannot provide the answer to the question of origins, because no scientist living today was present at the beginning. Lee stated, "In science men have not found the. . . answer to the question of suffering and death, no forgiveness for men's sins, no healing for the broken heart, no power to take the pain out of parting and the sting out of death, the gloom out of the grave" (*Top Ten* 141-42).

Read and study good writings on the evidences of Christianity. There is much old writing available that has never been surpassed in this field of study. There is also valuable current writing published regularly. With an honest heart, drink deeply from the wells of Christian evidences. You will know "the words of truth and reason" (Acts 26:25), and your faith will grow exceedingly (2 Thess. 1:3).

THE EXISTENCE OF GOD AND TERRORISM

In the prosecution of the Nuremburg trials, following World War II, the German Nazis were tried for the heinous crime of torturing and murdering six million Jewish men, women, and children. In his closing address, Robert H. Jackson, a Justice of the U.S. Supreme Court, and one of the Nuremburg prosecutors, argued that the Nazis were being tried by a "higher law" which "transcends the provincial and transient." (Warren and Flew 41). A higher law which transcends "the provincial" means it is not merely the law of any geographical area (i.e. America, Russia, Germany, etc.). To say it is a law which transcends "the transient" means it is above any law that has been passed by human beings during a certain period of time. In other words, the Nuremburg prosecutors affirmed that the Nazis were judged by a law which was (is) beyond any geographical area of the earth and beyond any period in human history.

We have heard our President, and others, speak of the ***evil*** acts perpetrated against civilization on September 11, 2001, and that those who did such are ***evildoers***. If such acts really were ***evil*** (and they were), and if those who did them can rightly be called ***evildoers*** (and they can), then there must be an objective reference by which human behavior is evaluated. Justice Jackson stated, ***"... a higher law."*** What is this "higher law?" It is the Ultimate Good who is God. Therefore, God exists. If such is not the case, then the horrific acts of September 11 were not acts of evil, and those who did them were not evildoers. Surely no right thinking person believes such! "The fool has said in his heart, 'There is no God'" (Psalm 14:1).

NO ATHEISTS IN COAL MINES

What would it be like to be trapped for 77 hours in a mine pit 240 feet underground? Additionally, imagine, that while you were in this pit, 60 million gallons of water came rushing through at a speed of 60-70 MPH. Such was the experience of nine coal miners at the Quecreek Mine in rural western Pennsylvania. And, in a rescue that transfixed the nation, all nine miners were pulled to safety three days after they became trapped underground when they inadvertently broke into an abandoned water-filled mine, which, according to maps, was supposed to have been 300 feet away.

Surely there is a sense in which no one but the Lord and these nine miners could really know what that nightmarish scene was like. I have heard their reports of what went on as they fought for their survival during those 77 hours, but I cannot comprehend. However, I am reminded again of how the Bible is so remarkably relevant to every crisis which we humans may face as we live life on Earth. Just when one might think that here is such a unique and unusual circumstance in life–a crisis so different from anything in our experience–the Bible declares, "Save me, O God! For the waters have come up to my neck. I sink in deep mire, where there is no standing; I have come into deep waters, where the floods overflow me. . . Let not the flood overflow me, nor let the deep swallow me up; And let not the pit shut its mouth on me" (Psalm 69:1-2, 15).

I do not know if any of these nine miners had knowledge of the above biblical passage. I do know they thought about, and talked about, God during those horrifying hours spent underground. To a man, I have heard them say, in interviews following their rescue, that their experience was a reminder of how there has to be "a higher power." It has been said, "There are no atheists in foxholes." It seems there are no atheists in coal mines either!

THE BIBLE AND THE SEARS CATALOG

A number of years ago I taught a class on church history. At the conclusion of the study, the class made a tour of various sites in Kentucky associated with the restoration of New Testament Christianity during the nineteenth and early twentieth centuries. One of the sites visited was the Lexington Theological Seminary. This institution, when it began, was known as The College of the Bible and, for some years, was a citadel for emphasis on, and loyalty to, the Bible. J. W. McGarvey was its leading personality and most influential teacher for many years. However, the Disciples of Christ (Christian Church) gained control of this institution, and its history since then has been one of a continual plunge into the depths of theological liberalism. This was illustrated when I, during our tour, asked the Librarian of the Seminary, "Do your faculty members subscribe to a doctrinal policy regarding the inspiration and inerrancy of the Bible?" In response he shouted, "No! There are things in the Bible that are not as true as things you read in the Sears Roebuck Catalog!"

After publishing it for more than 100 years, Sears ceased publication of its catalog. However, the Bible lives on. Regardless of the blasphemous attacks of unbelief, there is a Book that will outlive the Sears Catalog (and every other book). It never grows out of date. It withstands the assaults made against it. The Word of the Lord endures forever (2 Tim. 3:14-17; 1 Pet. 1:24-25)!

THE BIBLE: WHAT IS IT?

Old books often yield great treasures. The following tribute to the Bible is an example.

> This collection of books has taken such a hold on the world as no other. The literature of Greece, which goes up like incense from that land of temples and heroic deeds, has not half the influence of this book from a nation alike despised in ancient and modern times. It is read of a Sabbath in all the ten thousand pulpits of our land. In all the temples of Christendom is its voice lifted up, week by week. The sun never sets on its gleaming page. It goes equally to the cottage of the plain man and the palace of the king. It is woven into the literature of the scholar, and colours the talk of the street. The bark of the merchant cannot sail without it; no ship of war goes to the conflict but the Bible is there. It enters men's closets; mingles in all the grief and cheerfulness of life. The affianced maiden prays to God in Scripture for strength in her new duties; men are married by Scripture. The Bible attends them in their sickness; when the fever of the world is on them. The aching head finds a softer pillow when the Bible lies underneath. . . It goes with the peddler in his crowded pack; cheers him at even-tide, when he sits down dusty and fatigued. . . The timid man, about awaking from the dream of life, looks through the glass of Scripture, and his eye grows bright. . ." (Morris 5-6).

The Bible is beyond all other books as a river is beyond a drop of water. "My heart stands in awe of Your word" (Psalm 119:161).

SEVEN WONDERS OF THE WORD

Most have heard about "The Seven Wonders of the World." More need to hear about the wonders of *the Word* (the Bible). The Psalmist prayed, "Open my eyes, that I may see wondrous things from Your law" (Psalm 119:18). Again, he declared, "Your testimonies are wonderful. . ." (Psalm 119:129). I am impressed with the following seven wonders of the Word:

1. The wonder of its **INSPIRATION**! Not just part of it–not just the thoughts of it–but "ALL Scripture is given by inspiration of God" (2 Tim. 3:16). To the very ***jot*** (the tiniest letter) and ***tittle*** (the tiniest projection which distinguishes one letter from another), it is inspired (Matt. 5:18).

2. The wonder of its **FORMATION** ! It did not all come at once but over a period of some 1600 years. ". . . Precept upon precept, line upon line, here a little, there a little" (Isa. 28:10).

3. The wonder of its **UNIFICATION**! It is a library of 66 books, yet ONE BOOK. Written by some 40 writers over approximately 1600 years yet ONE MESSAGE (Rev. 19:10).

4. The wonder of its **REVELATION**! The Bible is the *complete*, *final* revelation of "the things of God" (1 Cor. 2:10-12) which came not by "the will of man" but as holy men of God were "moved by the Holy Spirit" (2 Pet. 1:20-21).

5. The wonder of its **INFORMATION**! It is the greatest literature in the world, but it is more–it contains "all things that pertain to life and godliness" (2 Pet. 1:3). No additional information is needed for it sufficiently equips man for every good work (2 Tim. 3:17).

6. The wonder of its **PROPAGATION**! It is read by all nations, classes, and races. It is the world's best seller.

7. The wonder of its **PRESERVATION**! The most hated of all books, yet it continues. "The word of the Lord endures forever" (1 Pet. 1:25).

THE LIGHT TO LEAD US HOME

A visit to a used book store uncovered a book lover's treasure (viz. a delightful volume published more than a quarter of a century ago and filled with thought-provoking anecdotes and capsules of wisdom). One tidbit of value was a story about an old preacher who, on foot, set out after the evening service to find his way along the edge of a dangerous cliff to the cottage where he was to spend the night. He had no lantern, and flashlights were then unknown. An old farmer, sensing the preacher's predicament, lighted a bundle of pine branches and handed it to the minister saying, "Take this, it will light your way home."

"But what if the wind blows it out?"

"It will see you home."

"But what if the rain extinguishes it?"

"It will see you home."

"But what if it burns out before I get there?"

"It will see you home."

And see him home it did (Havner 9-10).

Long ago the Psalmist said, "Your word is a lamp to my feet and a light to my path" (Psalms 119:105). There are times when theological smokescreeners try to hide the great doctrine of the Bible in the clouds and darkness of unbelief, but they are unable to invert its torch or quench one ray of its light.

The Bible may seem old-fashioned to those who are "ever learning and never able to come to the knowledge of the truth" (2 Tim. 3:7), yet man's little flashlights fail again and again, and the Bible keeps on glowing. The critics scorn it; cynics laugh at it; change agents dilute it. But the Bible–the Word of God–burns brightly. And it will see us home!

AN OLD BOOK AND THE BOOK

Many years ago, an annual used-book sale in Parkersburg, West Virginia, yielded a rare treasure. There, on a shelf surrounded by thousands of books on various and sundry topics, was *An Examination of the Alleged Discrepancies of the Bible* published in 1874 by John W. Haley. I quickly opened the book to see the price. Twenty-five cents!!! SOLD! I felt like a little boy with his special toy on Christmas morning.

In 1951, the late B.C. Goodpasture, longtime editor of the *Gospel Advocate*, described Haley's *Alleged Discrepancies Of The Bible* as "the most useful work of its kind." In The PREFACE, Haley humbly set forth his purpose for authoring this classic volume. He wrote, "If it shall help to vindicate the Bible from the reproaches and misrepresentations of its enemies, and to solve doubts in the minds of honest inquirers, the author's object will have been attained" (vi).

Haley's closing statement in The PREFACE is, itself, worth more than great sums of money. Haley wrote:

> Finally, let it be remembered that the Bible is neither dependent upon nor affected by the success or failure of my book. Whatever may become of the latter, whatever may be the verdict passed upon it by an intelligent public, the BIBLE will stand. In the ages yet to be, when its present assailants and defenders are mouldering in the dust, and when their very names are forgotten, the sacred volume will be, as it has been during the centuries past, the guide and solace of unnumbered millions of our race (x).

A BACKYARD VISIT ABOUT GOD AND THE BIBLE

I once enjoyed "backyard" Springtime chat sessions with a neighbor. We usually discussed everything from the weather–to family–to politics–to religion. One day, the topic of faith in God entered our conversation. John, my neighbor, said, "Chuck, I know who my Maker is. I have a very strong faith in God." John was to be commended, because the Bible affirms, "His invisible attributes are clearly seen, being understood by the things that are made... so that they are without excuse" (Rom. 1:20).

However, following his statement about God, John said, "But I don't believe all those things in the Bible. It has been written by man, and rewritten." I asked John, "How many times have you read the Bible?" He hesitated, and answered, "I never have sat down and read it all the way through." I thought, "How tragic!" Even the skeptic Rousseau, a French writer (1712-1778) acknowledged, "I will confess to you farther that the majesty of the Scriptures strikes me with admiration... Is it possible that a book, at once so simple and sublime, should be merely the work of man?" (qtd. in Mitchell 425).

The Bible was written, not to cause people to doubt, but to produce faith in Jesus Christ (cf. Rom. 1:16; 10:17). "These are written that you may believe that Jesus is the Christ, the Son of God..." (John 20:30-31). When one will read it slowly, frequently, and prayerfully, he will come to appreciate its greatness. Familiarity with the Bible will cause one to exclaim, "My heart stands in awe of Your word!" (Psalm 119:161).

THE BIBLE, NEW YORK, AND TIME OF WAR

During a trip to Pittsburgh for the purpose of receiving treatment at the University of Pittsburgh Medical Center, I had occasion to browse through some rare books in a bookstore located in an older section of the city. I came across a book, *The Bible In New York*, published in 1948. The terrorist attacks in New York, and the military response to those attacks, make the material in the aforementioned book extremely relevant and interesting. One of the book's chapters, "In Time Of War," tells about Scripture distribution to the armed forces during such major conflicts as World Wars I and II. Letters from presidents, generals, and other military leaders are cited which urged the troops to read the Bible and "seek from its pages strength... and assurance of life beyond the grave" (Fant 56).

One such letter, dated June 5, 1917, was from Colonel Theodore Roosevelt. It stated:

> The teachings of the New Testament are foreshadowed in Micah's verse: "What doth the Lord require of thee, but to do justly, and love mercy, and to walk humbly with thy God..." "Do justly": and therefore fight valiantly against the armies of Germany and Turkey for these nations in this crisis stand for the reign of Moloch, and Beelzebub on this earth... "Love mercy": treat prisoners well; succor the wounded; treat every woman as if she were your sister; care for the little children, and be tender with the old and helpless... "Walk humbly": you will do so if you study the life and teachings of the Savior... (63).

We are in a different time. Our troops are in a different war. But the same Book has the same message–Book divine in war and peace.

FACING THE 2000'S WITH THE "2000" YEAR-OLD BOOK

A cartoon pictured a man–Bible in hand–standing by a missile about to be launched. Above him a jet plane was soaring and, around him, scientists and technologists were running. In the midst of all this the man says, "Somehow I feel out of things!"

How can a book whose final parts were completed nearly 2000 years ago be relevant to life in the 2000's? Is it possible that this Book written centuries ago could be authoritative for the 21st century? What is there about this collection of ancient writings that would cause someone today to go to it for the answers to life's crucial questions?

The Bible is wonderful in its antiquity, but it never becomes antiquated even though its earliest portions antedate all other books. The tooth of time gnaws but makes no dent in the Bible. ***"Time writes no wrinkles on its brow."*** It is the very thing we need to face the 2000's. James Davis, former Secretary of Labor, summed up the world's condition as we face the 2000's and beyond: "The world never needed the Bible more than it does today" (*Top Ten* 46).

Incomparable–Inexhaustible–Indestructible. The Bible is the old-time Book, the new-time Book, and the all-time Book. In the words of the first line of A.Z. Conrad's classic poem: "Century follows century - There it stands!"

Sir Isaac Newton said: "If all the great books of the world were given life and were brought together in convention, the moment the Bible entered, the other books would fall on their faces, as the gods of Philistia fell when the ark of God was brought into their presence in the temple of Dagon" (48-49).

The Bible is the Book with which to face the 2000's, and beyond, because it is incomparable. There is none like it in its Messianic theme. The Person and Work of Jesus the Christ permeate the Bible from beginning (Gen. 3:15) to end (Rev. 22:20-21). His Person and Work are beyond human invention (cf. 2 Pet. 1:16). "No man ever spoke like this Man!" (John 7:46). His teaching remains incomparable. He is "the same yesterday, today, and forever" (Heb. 13:8).

The Bible is incomparable in its influence. It has traveled more highways, knocked at more doors, and spoken to more people in their native tongue than any book the world has ever known, can ever know, or will ever know. The great author, Walter Scott, requested, while on his death bed, that his son-in-law read to him. "From what book shall I read?" his son-in-law asked. Scott answered, "There is but one Book–the Bible" (Lockyer 109).

The Bible has been a safe guide through nineteen centuries plus, and it will safely guide through the 2000's and beyond. It is beyond all other books as a river is beyond a drop of water and a mountain is beyond a grain of sand!

Although its most recent parts were written more than 1900 years ago, the Bible is the one Book whose pages have never been exhausted. At the end of the nineteenth century R.A. Torrey wrote the following about the Bible:

> The human mind has been progressing through these eighteen centuries - we have outgrown every other book that belongs to the past, but so far from outgrowing the Bible we have not grown up to it. The Bible is not only up to date, but always ahead of date... If the Book were man's book we would have fathomed it centuries ago, but the fact that it has proved itself unfathomable for eighteen centuries is positive proof that in it are hidden the infinite treasures of the wisdom and knowledge of God... What a testimony to the divine origin of this Book that such infinite wisdom can be packed in so small a compass! The Bible is not such a very large Book (I have a copy that I carry in my vest pocket), but yet in a Book that can be printed in so small a compass there are packed away such treasures of wisdom that eighteen centuries of study by the world's best minds have been unable to exhaust it. How are we to account for it? There is no one

> but God who could pack such infinite treasures of truth in so small a compass (46-47).

What Torrey said near the end of the nineteenth century is still true in this century. As man faces the 2000's, the best minds of science and technology have not exhausted the Bible. "Your judgments are a great deep" (Psalm 36:6). The inexhaustible depth of the Bible will take us through the 2000's and beyond.

Hall Caine, late nineteenth and early twentieth century English novelist, once said, "There is no book in the world like it, and the finest novels ever written fall far short in interest of any one of the stories it tells. Whatever strong situations I have in my books are not my creation, but are taken from the Bible" (qtd. in Sweeney 357). It is still true today that the Bible is superior to all other books. In it the historian has found his most thrilling chapters, the poet his greatest themes, the orator his most beautiful quotations, and the preacher his divine message.

The Genesis account of creation is superior to all other accounts of origins. Genesis One has been used as an example of sublimity in writing. The story of Ruth in the Old Testament has been said to be greater than anything in the classics. Proverbs is marvelously thorough, yet simple. It is the most superb practical wisdom on everyday life that can be found anywhere. Job is the greatest treatise available on the problem of human suffering. The Book of Psalms contains the greatest devotional literature ever written. There is hardly one human emotion left untouched in the Psalms.

An atheist mailed a Christian some literature which attacked the Bible. The Christian replied: "My Dear Sir, if you have anything better than the Sermon on the Mount, the story of the prodigal son, and the good Samaritan... or if you can suggest anything more consoling than the 23rd Psalm, or if you can supply anything which will throw more light on the future and reveal a Father more merciful and kind than the New Testament does, please send it to me." There was no reply.

As we face the 2000's, it is a wonder that the Bible is yet with us. No book has been the object of more challenges, opposition, and misrepresentation. Great infidels like Celsus, Voltaire, Hume, Paine, and Ingersol made it a fixed purpose of life to attack and destroy the Bible "but the word of the Lord endures forever" (1 Pet. 1:25). Jesus said, "Heaven and earth will pass away but My words will by no means pass away" (Matt. 24:35).

R.G. Lee eloquently summarized:

> He that sitteth in the heavens shall laugh at those who think they destroy His Word and its triumphs. Voltaire cut not one twig from its great forest. Paine drowned not one page nor one word of any page in his infidel ink. Ingersol, with intent to kill, shortened not its life by one hour. Diocletian broke not one string on its harp of ten thousand strings. Agnostics who kindled their bonfires upon it burned away not one thread of its garments. Atheists have not been able to steal one flower from is gorgeous flower gardens. Unbelieving scientists, with microscope and telescope and test-tube, have not been able to dilute one drop of its sweetness... The Bible is still the Book... that fans us in our faintness, guides us in our gloom, helps us in our hazards, directs us in our doubts, prompts us in our perplexities (*Top Ten* 48-49).

Give me the Bible in the 2000's, and beyond, unto eternity!

FROM ETERNITY TO BETHLEHEM

Two thousand years ago, a baby, whose name was Jesus, was born in Bethlehem of Judea. The world has never been the same. Times change. Habits change. Nations forget their history. They never forget Jesus of Nazareth.

Jesus really was born, lived, died, resurrected and ascended. These are historical facts. However, there is a sense in which we need to be careful as we speak of Jesus Christ as an "historical person." You see, the Person who was (is) Jesus, not only lived as an historical Person, but He has *always* existed.

Some 700 years before Jesus was born, the prophet Micah stated: "But you, Bethlehem Ephrathah, though you are little among the thousands of Judah, yet out of you shall come forth to Me the One to be Ruler in Israel Whose goings forth are from old, from everlasting" (Micah 5:2). Observe that this One described as coming from Bethlehem to be Ruler in Israel is One whose "goings forth are from long ago from days of eternity" (NASV). E. B. Pusey wrote: "Here words, denoting eternity and used of the eternity of God, are united together to impress the belief of the Eternity of God, the Son" (70).

Here we have the existence of the Messiah before His birth in time and space. He who would be born in Bethlehem was already in existence–during it, before it, and through all eternity. Jesus who was from everlasting, the Ancient of Days, became the infant of days!

"In the beginning was the Word, and the Word was with God, and the Word was God. He was in the beginning with God. All things were made through Him, and without Him nothing was made that was made" (John 1:1-3). Here are some of the most profound verses in all the Bible. They take the reader from Bethlehem (John 1:14) back to eternity. The term *was* (verse one) is from the Greek word ***en*** and, "used in all three clauses of this verse, is expressive in each case of *continuous timeless existence*" (Bernard 2). It is descriptive of continuous action in past time. In other words, in the beginning He already existed and had been existing before the beginning.

As to designation, John says He was the Word–the Word behind which there is thought, purpose and reason. As to relationship, John says He was with God. This involves working with interaction. As to His nature and essence, John says He was God. Here is deity and equality with God (cf. Philip. 2:5-6). As to His relationship with the physical world, John says that everything came into existence through Him, and apart from Him nothing came into existence. The Greek construction here shows *indirect* agency. The Father was the direct agent, and the Word (Who became Jesus of Nazareth) was the indirect agent (cf. 1 Cor. 8:6; Col. 1:13-17; Heb. 1:2). Before Bethlehem–when the morning stars serenaded the advent of the infant Earth–He placed His signature on every page of creation. Before He rested on the bosom of a mother without an earthly father, He rested on the bosom of the Father without a mother (Lee, *Top Ten* 112).

One of the great statements in the Sacred Scriptures, which implies the marvelous, glorified, pre-existent state of our Lord prior to Bethlehem, is the following: "For you know the grace of our Lord Jesus Christ, that though He was rich, yet for your sakes He became poor..." (2 Cor. 8:9). When was Jesus rich? Certainly not at Bethlehem or thereafter on Earth. He was born in a borrowed stable, rowed the Sea of Galilee in a borrowed boat, fed the multitudes with borrowed food, rode into Jerusalem on a borrowed beast, ate His last meal in a borrowed room, and was buried in a borrowed tomb! As Bernard states concerning the aforementioned statement by Paul: "There is nowhere in St. Paul a more definite statement of his belief in the pre-existence of Christ before His incarnation" (*Second Corinthians* 87).

He was rich in glory with the Father (John 17:5) before all things (Col. 1:17), when He made all things (John 1:3), when, as the

Rock, He followed Israel and gave her spiritual drink (1 Cor. 10:4), and when He inspired the revelation of the prophets who spoke of Him (1 Pet. 1:10-12). But then came Bethlehem–and He became poor that through His poverty we might become rich. Milton (qtd. in Lee, *Grapes* 11) wrote:

That glorious form, that light insufferable,
And that far-beaming blaze of majesty,
Wherewith he wont at heaven's high council-table,
To sit the midst of trinal unity.
He laid aside, and here with us to be,
Forsook the courts of everlasting day,
And chose with us a darksome house of clay.
— John Milton

"And the word became flesh..." (John 1:14). The word *became* in this verse is a verb denoting the commencement of human existence in time. It is contrasted with the verb *was* (John 1:1) which is a verb of continual timeless existence.

THE WORD BECAME FLESH... He who had eternal pre-existence became what He was not in eternity, viz. flesh. He came down from the heights of Deity to the depths of humanity (cf. Philip. 2:5-7; Heb. 1:8; 2:17). He who was the Ancient of Days became the infant of days. He created the angels (Col. 1:16), but was made a little lower than the angels (Heb. 2:9). He could say, "Before Abraham was, I am" (John 8:58), yet He was born two thousand years after Abraham. He made woman from the side of man (Gen. 2:22; John 1:3), but was wrapped in swaddling cloths by a woman's hands and laid in a manger "because there was no room for them in the inn" (Luke 2:7).

His birth into the world by a virgin was a translation as well as an incarnation. It was a transfer of His Person from an eternal existence beyond time and space to an existence measured in time and space. In fact, so significant is this event that the date lines of all nations are bent around His manger cradle. History is HIS-STORY! "Thanks be to God for His indescribable gift!" (2 Cor. 9:15).

THE PALACE AND THE STABLE

From April 1 to April 22, 1923, twenty-three sermons were delivered by the inimitable N.B. Hardeman at the famed Ryman Auditorium, home of the Grand Ole Opry, in Tennessee's capital city of Nashville. The second of these sermons included an examination of the period between the Old and New Testaments in which Hardeman surveyed the reign of the infamous Herod the Great who occupied the throne when the angel of the Lord announced on that starlit night, that a Savior, Christ the Lord, had been born (Luke 2:8, 11). Hardeman affirmed:

> If ever evil was embodied in one man, it was in that corrupt mass that lay upon the royal bed and plotted death even when incarnate love was born into the world.
>
> From the couch of Herod pass for a moment to the cradle of Christ. A peasant couple from the hills of Galilee trudged along to the historic Bethlehem, the woman worn with long hard travel and pinched with the pain of approaching maternity... It was late in the day ere they reached the "inn", and all the sleeping compartments were occupied. A place was found on the lower level used for the stabling of the cattle, and there on that night, Jesus, the Christ was born.
>
> Such a contrast between the village khan and the palace fortress the world has never seen... The Prince of Peace was among the beasts, and the beast was among the princes. The real King was in the stable, while the usurper was clad in purple... (53-54).

Twenty centuries of human history have not diminished the power of the cradled Christ.

THE PERFECT CHARACTER OF CHRIST

Three times Pilate said, "I find no fault in Him" (John 18:38; 19:4, 6). It is a reminder that the more one truly gets to know Jesus Christ the more reverence he can have for His character. The measure of His life and character is summarized in the report of Mark who wrote, "They were astonished beyond measure, saying 'He has done all things well'" (Mark 7:37).

Ernest Renan, nineteenth century linguistic scholar, who wrote extensively on early Christianity, published his most famous work, *The Life of Jesus*, in 1863. He dismissed Christ as a fanatical and deluded religious leader. He argued that the resurrection of Jesus was nothing more than a rumor propagated by Christ's followers to keep His memory alive. And yet, Renan concluded his book by saying, ". . . Jesus will not be surpassed... All the ages will proclaim that among the sons of men there is none born who is greater than Jesus" (227).

In an 1889 volume, which is a classic work on the deity of Christ, another wrote:

> The facts of His humanity and of His work and influence in the world forbid us to classify Jesus with men, and the recognition of His divinity alone explains the facts of His humanity. Considered as God-man all is in harmony; miracles take their proper place in the records of His history, and mind and nature, heaven and earth, God and man meet in Jesus, the Christ. But —if He be only a man — He is such a man as were a thousand times worth dying for and following forever, through time and eternity (Haygood 60).

Truly, this Man is the Son of God!

LAID IN A MANGER–NAILED TO A CROSS

Jesus was born with the shadow of the cross upon Him. His birth was announced by the angel who said, "There is born to you this day in the city of David a Savior, who is Christ the Lord" (Luke 2:11). As significant as His birth was, it was in His death that the power to procure our salvation (i.e. His blood) was operative. Paul wrote, "... While we were still sinners, Christ died for us. Much more then, having now been justified by His blood, we shall be saved..." (Rom. 5:8-9). In the shadow of the cross, He learned to walk; He learned to talk; and He learned to work.

Once, in the city of London, a little girl was lost. She was in tears, because she could not tell the police her address. They named several landmarks, but none of them helped her recognize her home. Then someone mentioned the cross and the great stone across the road. Her tears ceased. She dried her eyes and said, "Yes, take me to the cross!"

TAKE ME TO THE CROSS! The way of the cross leads home. To find home we must go to the cross. It is good to go to Bethlehem but, to reach home, we must go to Calvary. One of the dangers in the season of the year known as Christmas is that many go to Bethlehem but never make it to Calvary.

Near the Cross! O Lamb of God,
Bring its scenes before me;
Help me walk from day to day,
With its shadow o'er me!
— Fanny J. Crosby

Several hundred years ago on the southern coast of China, on a hill overlooking a harbor, Portuguese settlers built a large cathedral for worship. Sometime afterwards the cathedral was destroyed by a typhoon. For years, the cathedral remained in ruins with no part of it standing except a high front wall. High atop this wall was a huge bronze cross. In 1825, Sir John Bowring saw the cross atop the wall on the distant hill. The cross, as a focal point, so impressed Bowring that he was motivated to write the following familiar words (Osbeck 121):

In the cross of Christ I glory,
Tow'ring O'er the wrecks of time;
All the light of sacred story
Gathers round its head sublime.
— John Bowring

When the angel of the Lord announced the birth of Jesus "there was with the angel a multitude of the heavenly host praising God and saying: 'Glory to God in the highest. . .'" (Luke 2:14). The glory of God was revealed in that manger in Bethlehem. However, it was manifested even greater in Calvary's cross. All we have, and all we shall have, was bought for us by the blood of the Son of God. "God forbid that I should glory except in the cross" (Gal. 6:14).

Joseph and Mary brought "the Child Jesus, to do for Him according to the custom of the law" (Luke 2:27; cf. Lev. 12:1-6). There was a man in Jerusalem whose name was Simeon who was eagerly awaiting the day when he could see the Messiah (Luke 2:25-26). When Simeon saw the baby "he took him up in his arms and blessed God" (Luke 2:28-32). He said to Mary, "Behold, this child is destined for the fall and rising of many in Israel, and for a sign which will be spoken against" (Luke 2:34).

This prophecy announced by Simeon is marvelously linked to the cross of Christ. Jesus would be like a stone over which some would trip, fall, and perish, but by which others would be enabled to rise and be saved (cf. Rom 11:9 ff; 1 Pet. 2:6-8). Those who imagine themselves to be strong and high, who rely on their own merit and power, will come to a woeful undoing, because they do not realize their need for the cross, and they do not take refuge in the Christ. Those who bend low at the foot of the cross, and obey the gospel, will be raised up with the hope of eternal life (Rom. 6:1-11, 23).

Just as Simeon had predicted, when the nails penetrated Jesus' flesh and the spear pierced His side, a sword pierced His mother's soul (Luke 2:35). But a door opened, which is wide enough, to let a guilty world go out into the sunshine of satisfied divine justice and into the light of the countenance of God (1 John 2:1-2).

Paul wrote, "Thanks be unto God for His unspeakable gift!" (2 Cor. 9:15, KJV). The word translated *unspeakable (inexpressible,* RSV; *indescribable*, NKJ) is from the Greek word ***anekdiegto***. How fitting that this word appears only once in the Greek New Testament. The gift of God's only Son is a one-of-a-kind gift. The cross of Christ stands uniquely on the shores of time drawing the inhabitants of human history to its unfathomable properties.

As one unnamed writer eloquently stated:

> The history of human guilt culminates in the cross. The purposes of divine love are made intelligible at the cross. The rays of glory emanating from Christ are focused in the cross. The fingers of prophecy point to the cross. The mysteries of prophecy are unraveled at the cross. The great problem of human redemption is solved at the cross. The serpent's head is bruised at the cross. The foundation of salvation is unsealed at the cross. The streams of civilization AND all the great events of the gospel yield in importance to the cross. The transfiguration foreshadowed the cross. The resurrection was the complement of the cross. Pentecost was the fruit of the cross. Bethlehem and Nazareth, Galilee, and Jerusalem, Tabor and Olivet, gleam only in the light of the cross. All the great doctrines of grace revolve around the cross. Earthly glory fades at the cross. Intellect is sanctified at the cross. Sin dies at the cross. Slave chains are snapped at the cross. The bitters of life are sweetened at the cross. The shadows of death are dispelled at the cross. The heaven of the redeemed is built upon the cross. The darkness of eternity is irradiated at the cross. Hallelujah for the cross (qtd. in Lee, *Grapes* 28).

TEN REASONS WHY I BELIEVE HE WAS RAISED

The resurrection of Jesus of Nazareth is the "Rock of Gibraltar" of the Christian faith. It is the solid foundation of our hope (1 Pet. 3:15). The following are ten reasons why I believe in the resurrection of Jesus of Nazareth:

1. For the same reason I believe that George Washington lived and was the First President of the United States. It is an historical fact (Acts 1:3; 1 Cor. 15:3-4).
2. Because it has been reported by eyewitnesses (Luke 1:1-4; Acts 2:32).
3. Because of the changed lives of the twelve apostles of Christ (Mark 14:31, 50; Acts 4:13, 18-20).
4. Because of the conversion of Saul of Tarsus (Acts 7:58; 8:1; 22:3-5; 26:19-25; Gal. 1:23).
5. Because the enemies of it could not disprove it, even though they possessed the motivation and power to do such (Matt. 27:62-66; 28:11-15; Acts 4:16).
6. Because of the church of Christ (Matt. 16:18).
7. Because of the Lord's Day (Mark 16:9; Acts 20:7).
8. Because of the Lord's Supper (Acts 2:42; 20:7).
9. Because of baptism (Rom. 6:3-5).
10. Because of the consequences of not believing (1 Cor. 15:13-19).

Lord Chief Justice of England, Lord Darling, once said that "no intelligent jury in the world could fail to bring in a verdict that the resurrection story is true" (qtd. in Green 54). Case closed! He lives!!!

AN ENGLISHMAN AND THE CONVERSION OF SAUL

George Lyttelton was born at Worcestershire, England, January 17, 1709. He died in 1773 at the age of sixty-four. He belonged to a distinguished family. The name of George Lyttelton was seen in every account of debate in the House of Commons. The eighteenth century was the darkest period religiously in the history of England since the Reformation. It was the age of the great agnostics, rationalists, and unbelievers. Like so many of the literary men of his time, George Lyttelton was led at first to reject the Christian religion.

Fully persuaded that the Bible was an imposture, Lyttelton was determined to expose it. He chose the conversion of Paul and his friend, Gilbert West, chose the resurrection of Christ for the subject of his hostile criticism (cf. *Observations on the History and Evidences of the Resurrection of Jesus Christ).* Both Lyttelton and West sat down to their respective tasks. The result of their separate attempts was that they were both converted by their efforts to overthrow Christianity!

West and Lyttelton came together, not as they expected to exult over an imposture, but to lament over their folly and affirm the Bible is the Word of God. Their able inquiries have provided two of the most valuable treatises in the realm of Christian Evidences. In the opening paragraph of his work, Lyttelton wrote: "The conversion (of Saul) was itself a demonstration sufficient to prove Christianity to be a divine revelation" (Bales 106). Lyttelton's matchless argument has been a blessing to thousands of doubting souls who have come to know "those things which are most surely believed among us" (Luke 1:1).

"BELIEVE YOUR MOTHER"

Many years ago I came across a brief treatise on the evidences in favor of Christianity and the divine authorship of the Bible, which is entitled, *The Bible True, and Infidelity Wicked.* It was authored by Wm. S. Plumer and published by the American Tract Society with no publishing date recorded. It shows the wear of many years and likely was published in the late 1800's. In spite of its brevity (only seventy-nine pages), it is a storehouse of information which can strengthen faith. As an example of such, I cite the following incident as recorded in its pages:

> Colonel Ethan Allen of New England was an officer in the war of American Independence. He was brave, he was patriotic, he was gifted, he was an infidel. Having fought the enemies of his country, he made war on the Lamb, and wrote with much subtlety a work against Christianity. He was also a husband and a father. . . In the course of time an interesting daughter was taken sick. It soon became apparent to her physician, her parents, and herself, that she had but a short time to live. In these solemn circumstances she made an appeal to her father, an infidel, and to her mother, a Christian, not to deceive her, but to tell her whether she should believe the infidel or Christian system. The mother, from emotion or from prudence, was silent. In the father, parental love gained the ascendancy over infidel passion and prejudice, and he said, "My daughter, believe your mother. She has told you the truth" (77-78).

We search the world for truth;
We cull the good, the pure, the beautiful
from all old flower fields of the soul;
And weary seekers of the best,
We come back laden from our quest
To find that all the sages said
Is in the book our mothers read.
— *Whittier*

HAVE YOU ANY HOPE IN DEATH?

My attention has often been arrested by the many contrasts between the death of the unrighteous and the death of the faithful child of God. The writer of Proverbs presented this contrast when he wrote: "The wicked is banished in his wickedness, but the righteous has a refuge (hath hope, KJV) in his death" (Prov. 14:32). Many have been the incidents which have illustrated this great truth.

One illustration of such was manifested in a conversation which occurred on the beautiful hills at a place not far from where this is being written. The conversation took place in the early 1800's at what is now Bethany, West Virginia (Brooke County). The conversants were Robert Owen, noted skeptic of the nineteenth century, and Alexander Campbell, gospel preacher. Owen and Campbell were at Bethany, Campbell's home, planning their upcoming debate. One day, as they were out walking while discussing plans for the debate, they came to Campbell's family cemetery. Owen stopped, turned to Campbell and said, "There is one advantage I have over the Christians–I am not afraid to die. Most Christians have fear in death, but if some few items of my business were settled, I should be perfectly willing to die at any moment."

Campbell then answered, "You say you have no fear in death: have you any ***hope*** in death?" After a solemn pause Owen answered, "No." "Then," rejoined Campbell (pointing to an ox standing near), "You are on the level of that brute. He has fed till he is satisfied, and stands in the shade whisking off the flies, and has neither hope nor fear in death" (Richardson 242-243).

Christianity provides the most sensible, rewarding way to live now, but it also looks beyond, takes the gloom out of the grave, and gives a hope steadfast and sure.

"THERE WILL BE NO SINGING"

Robert Ingersoll was a renowned agnostic who lived during the 19th century. His philosophy was summarized with the words, "The Bible is a Delusion." On November 29, 1896, *The New York Journal* presented a caricature of Ingersoll and stated, "Ingersoll illustrated the ever increasing boldness and audacity of doubt as to the Christian faith. . ." (qtd. in Sweeting 100).

Ingersoll was a naturalist, having no time for anything besides the here and now. He taught:

> Secularism is the religion of humanity. It embraces the affairs of this world. . . . It is a declaration of intellectual independence. . . . It means living for. . . the present instead of the past; for this world instead of the next. . . . It does not believe in praying and receiving, but in earning and deserving (100).

Ingersoll was called upon to speak at the funeral of his brother. Standing by his departed brother's grave, this most noted infidel said, "Life is a narrow vale between the cold and barren peaks of two eternities. We strive in vain to look beyond the heights. We cry aloud and the only answer is the echo of our wailing cry" (Russell 247-48).

Robert Ingersoll died suddenly July 21, 1899. The news of his death shocked the family. His body was kept at home several days because of his wife's reluctance to part with it. It was eventually removed because the health of the family was at stake. His remains were cremated. Sweeting wrote, ". . . the public response to his passing was that of hopelessness" (100). The memorial service included the notice, "THERE WILL BE NO SINGING." Wonder why?

"THE SWEET RETURN OF SPRING"

I came across an old (1856) two volume set of books entitled, *Sacred Philosophy of the Seasons.* The author is Henry Duncan, and the object of these volumes is to demonstrate the existence and attributes of God, in various phenomena of the revolving year. Each of the volumes contains two sections representing two of the four seasons (Spring/Summer and Fall/Winter). Each of these sections presents an argument complete in itself, and peculiar to the season it treats.

Concerning Spring, Duncan wrote:

> Spring has been celebrated in glowing terms by the poets of all ages. . . The *gradual* progress of Spring indicates beneficent design. . . Were the change from winter to spring to be sudden, the constitution of organized existences, such as we find it in our own latitude, would receive so violent an impulse, as would be attended with many injurious consequences. . . When we observe the earth *gradually* exchanging its winter robes for a mantle of liveliest green, the flowers springing up in fresh luxuriance at our feet, and every shrub, and tree putting forth is buds, which are beautifully wonder and delight. . . The sweet return of Spring. . . But need we wonder. . . seeing it is but in accordance with all the operations of the Great Supreme" (*Spring* 9, 13, 14, 18).

Truly, ". . . He did not leave Himself without witness. . . He did good, gave us. . . fruitful seasons. . ." (Acts 14:17).

THE FALL OF THE LEAF

The Bible contains impressive images drawn from the leaves. Job likened himself to "a leaf driven to and fro" (Job 13:25). Isaiah wrote that some are like "an oak whose leaf fadeth" (Isa. 1:30, ASV). And though the man of faith is "like a tree. . . whose leaf also shall not wither" (Psalm 1:3), there is a sense in which "we all fade as a leaf" (Isa. 64:6).

Pause, and behold the state of the trees in late autumn. Apply the lessons impressively taught. As Duncan wisely urged:

> Linger awhile amidst the bared and melancholy woods, now tossing in the cold winds of October. . . As trees of every kind, and in every locality, lose their leaves, so all nations and families fleet rapidly away... The vigorous youth, the full-formed man, and the old man bowing under his years, are equally withered by the blast of death... If some leaves, also, are not violently snatched from their boughs by the freezing gale, the surer process of natural decay at length effects their fall, and they at last follow their decaying predecessors. Thus again it is with man. The violence of various accidents, fire and flood, war, famine and pestilence, or the diseases which he brings on himself, or inherits, cuts off most of his race, many of them in the full prime of their days. If a few, escaping all these casualties, remain behind in their homes, they are only like the last leaves upon the bough... Surely the race of man is frail and fleeting as the leaves! (*Autumn* 362-363).

Although the fall of the leaf reminds us of our mortality and death, we behold Him Who is "the resurrection and the life" (John 11:25). He takes the gloom out of the grave and gives us a hope that is steadfast and sure! Every Lord's Day is a memorial of this hope.

CHRISTIANITY AND DEATH

The Bible affirms, "It is appointed for men to die once . . ." (Heb. 9:27). This is true for every man on Earth, in every place on Earth, during every period of history on Earth. Unless the Lord returns before, it is true for each one that "his day shall come to die" (1 Sam. 26:10). It is "the common fate of all men" (Num. 16:29). It has been correctly quipped that the statistics are that "one out of one dies." In a good book which was written several years ago, Loraine Boettner observed:

> There is a tendency on the part of many people to avoid any serious discussion or even thought on the subject of death. Yet every person knows that in the normal course of events sooner or later that experience will happen to him. Every community has its cemetery. Nothing is more certain about life than the fact of death. It may be long delayed, but it will surely come . . . Heart attacks, and other diseases, accidents, wars, fires, etc., have taken their toll. Death is no respecter of persons. It may come to anyone, young or old, rich or poor, saint or sinner, at any time, or any place. And when God calls, none can escape, nor excuse, nor alibi that appointment (9).

Death is the appointment we can all bank on keeping. It is inevitable. It may come early in life or years later. But, come it will. And the only way to escape is to never be born.

In his work entitled, *The Bible on the Life Hereafter*, originally published in 1959, William Hendriksen discussed some attitudes toward death that should be avoided (32-33). We cannot ultimately avoid death (Heb. 9:27), but we can avoid wrong attitudes toward death. Some of these attitudes include the following: 1. ESCAPISM. Escapism avoids even the mention of death. Louis XV forbid his servants to mention death in his presence. In our own culture the word *death* is often evaded. If death is discussed at all, it is often the case that other words and phrases are substituted for it. 2. FATALISM. The fatalist attempts to make himself, and others, believe that he is not afraid of death. His attitude toward death is, "So what?" 3. PESSIMISM. The pessimist wearies of life and gives in to suicide. At least every three minutes a suicide occurs in the U.S., and it has been estimated that for every suicide there are eight unsuccessful suicide attempts. Such loses sight of the infinite value of human life (cf. Gen. 9:6) and of the God in Whom we live, and move, and have our being (Acts 17:28).

Christianity provides the way to overcome these hopeless, helpless, and hapless views of life and death. Christianity's view of death is superior to all other philosophies and religions. This is seen in the pictures of hope painted on the sacred canvas of the Holy Scriptures. For the Christian, death means (1) rest, (2) release, (3) reunion, (4) return, and (5) reward.

REST. John wrote, "Blessed are the dead who die in the Lord... that they may rest from their labors..." (Rev. 14:13). Death is sometimes set forth in the Bible as *sleep* (cf. John 1:11; Acts 7:59-60; 1 Thess. 4:14). This is used figuratively to describe the state of the body in death. That part of man which sleeps in death is in the dust (Dan. 12:2). Only the body "goes to the dust" at death (Eccl. 12:7). Therefore, the figure of death as sleep describes the body, not the soul or spirit, of man. The Bible knows nothing of "soul sleep." This figure of sleep suggests (1) rest, (2) continuity of identity, i.e. the one who gets up in the morning following a night of rest is the same person who went to sleep the night before, and (3) the resurrection is implied, in that, when we are only sleeping, we will rise after awhile. The person remains conscious after death as the body returns to the elements of the earth while the resurrection is awaited (Luke 16:19-31; John 5:28-29).

RELEASE. Biblically, death is also referred to as a decease (Luke 9:31; 2 Pet. 1:5). *Decease* is from the Greek, ***exodos***, meaning departure. From this word we get the word *exit*. It also provides the title for the second book in the Bible (Exodus). The exodus of the Israelites did not result in their extinction. In fact, as they exited

Egypt, they were on their way to a better country (cf. Heb. 11:13-16). The word ***analusis*** (2 Tim. 4:6) also means departure. It was either a nautical term, depicting a ship setting sail, or a term of the military with reference to the break up of an encampment (cf. 2 Cor. 5:1). For the Christian, death is departure for the glad plains of a never ending eternity where "Eden's morn shall dawn with sparkling dew."

REUNION. Biblically, death is pictured as a reunion with loved ones who have lived and died in faith. The death of Abraham is beautifully described in the following: "Then Abraham breathed his last and died in a good old age, an old man and full, and was gathered to his people" (Gen. 25:8). "Gathered to his people" does not refer to the burial of the body, because Abraham's body was buried near Mamre in Palestine, and his relatives were buried hundreds of miles away in other regions. The phrase refers to a reunion with loved ones after death (cf. 2 Sam. 12:23; Matt. 8:11; 1 Thess. 4:13-18).

RETURN. Death means being "absent from the body" (cf. James 2:26), and "at home with the Lord" (2 Cor. 5:8). The expression, "at home with the Lord," has reference to "one among his own people" as opposed to "one away from home" (Robertson 229). Here is the deeply touching picture of returning home "at the end of life's troublesome way."

REWARD. Jesus said to the penitent thief, "Today you will be with Me in Paradise" (Luke 23:43). Thus, Paul could say, "... to die is gain" (Philip. 1:21). One of the greatest preachers in the last century was B. C. Goodpasture. He died in 1977. On the morning that he suffered a fatal stroke, Goodpasture was reading from one of his favorite authors, John Henry Jowett. He circled a paragraph in his reading that morning which said: "And yet I must die. Yes, but the old enemy shall now be my friend... He will not be my master, but my servant. He shall just open the door into my Father's house of unspeakable blessedness and glory. Death shall *not* hurt us" (Henley 585). Thanks be to God Who gives us the victory over death through Jesus (1 Cor. 15:57)!

THE FATHERHOOD OF GOD

Several years ago I heard a great gospel preacher say, "If I were beginning my preaching ministry over, there are not many changes I would make, but one of the few I would make is I would preach more on the fatherhood of God." Truly, one of the great comforting doctrines of the Bible is the fatherhood of God. The fatherhood of God is revealed to some degree (though not completely) in the Old Testament. God is "a father of the fatherless" (Psalm 68:5). "As a father pities his children, so the Lord pities those who fear Him" (Psalm 103:13).

The doctrine of the fatherhood of God is fully revealed in the New Testament. Especially is it the case that in the gospels we see this great doctrine. The fatherhood of God is mentioned in Matthew 44 times, in Mark 5 times, in Luke 17 times, and in John 122 times. Nearly every chapter in John contributes in a powerful way toward the development of this theme (cf. 1:18; 2:17; 3:35; 4:23; 5:30; 6:57; 7:29; 8:19; 9:35-37; 10:15, 17; 11:41; 12:49-50; 13:1; 14:6, 9; 15:23; 16:15, 32; 17:4, 21; 18:11; 19:11; 20:25). From chapter one, where we read, "The only begotten Son, who is in the bosom of the Father, he has declared Him" (1:18), to the next to last chapter, when Jesus said, "... I am ascending to my Father and your Father..." (20:17), the fatherhood of God is emphasized.

There are four ways in which the Fatherhood of God is presented in the Scriptures:

1. God is Father in that He has created all. "He has made from one blood every nation of men..." (Acts 17:26), and He is "the Father of spirits" (Heb. 12:9).
2. God was a Father to the nation of Israel. He said, "I am a father to Israel . . ." (Jer. 31:9).
3. God is uniquely the Father of Jesus. "For God so loved the world that He gave His only begotten Son..." (John 3:16). Note also Hebrews 1:5.
4. God is the Father to those who are born into His spiritual family. Entrance into God's family–the church (Eph. 2:19; 1 Tim. 3:15) is presented in two

> figures. First, the process is set forth in the figure of a birth. One enters the kingdom of God through the birth of water and the Spirit (John 3:3-5; 1 Pet. 1:23). Secondly, the figure of adoption is used to picture entrance into God's family. "For you did not receive the spirit of bondage... but you received the Spirit of adoption (i.e. sonship) by whom we cry out, 'Abba, Father'" (Rom. 8:15; cf. Eph. 1:5). During slavery days, a group of Northerners were visiting New Orleans and observed a company of spiritless, indifferent slaves. However, one slave walked with his shoulders back and head erect. Someone asked, "Who is that fellow? Is he the straw boss or a slave owner?" The answer came, "No, he is just an old fool who cannot get it out of his head that he is the son of a king." As John wrote, "Behold what manner of love the Father has bestowed on us that we should be called children of God...!" (1John 3:1).

One of the reasons I know that fatherhood is great is because it teaches us great lessons about God. If it is the case that imperfect earthly fathers know how to give good gifts to their children, then it is the case that the perfect heavenly Father will give good things to His children (Matt. 7:7-11). The heavenly Father will provide physically for His children. If He feeds creatures (i.e. birds) that are lesser in value, then He will feed creatures (i.e. human beings) that are greater in value (Matt. 6:25-26). He knows our physical needs and will add these things to our lives as we put first things first (Matt. 6:32-33). The knowledge that we have such a Father should bring freedom from worry to our lives (Matt. 6:25-33).

The heavenly Father will provide spiritually for His children. He provides spiritual security (John 10:28-29; cf. Rom. 8:31-39). A group of botanists were exploring inaccessible regions of the Alps in search of new species of flowers. One day they discovered through field glasses a flower of rare beauty. However, the only way it could be reached was by someone being lowered into a deep ravine to get it. A native lad was offered a sum of money if he would allow himself to be lowered to pick the flower. He surveyed the situation and excused himself. Later he returned with an older man. The lad then said to the botanists, "I'll go over the cliff and retrieve the flower if you let this man hold the rope. He's my Dad." Thank God that we have earthly fathers to provide and protect, and thank God that we have Him to "hold the rope" when we are in distress (Psalm 18:6, 16).

Some fathers are able to leave great sums of money for their children to inherit. Whether one ever receives such an inheritance from an earthly father, he possesses, as a child of God, the hope of the greatest possible inheritance. Peter wrote, "Blessed be the God and Father of our Lord Jesus Christ, who according to His abundant mercy has begotten us again to a living hope through the resurrection of Jesus Christ from the dead, to an inheritance incorruptible and undefiled and that does not fade away, reserved in heaven for you..." (1 Pet. 1:3-4). Herein is an inheritance, based on one's relationship with the heavenly Father, which, in ultimate value, exceeds any earthly inheritance. Jesus affirmed, "In My Father's house are many mansions; if it were not so, I would have told you. I go to prepare a place for you" (John 14:2). Later, in the same context, Jesus stated, "I will not leave you orphans; I will come to you" (John 14:18). Although it seems to be the case that the coming of Jesus in verse eighteen is connected to the coming of the Holy Spirit to indwell the Christian (cf. John 14:16-17), the doctrine of the Fatherhood of God is also implied. The believer is not an orphan. He has a divine Father, and he possesses the hope of a wonderful inheritance.

The doctrine of the Fatherhood of God should affect how we live (cf. 2 Cor. 6:18-7:1). A Christian and his skeptical neighbor were discussing the evidences for the divine origin of Christianity. The skeptic asked the Christian, "If God is your Father, why do you live like an orphan?" John wrote, "Behold what manner of love the Father has bestowed on us, that we should be called children of God!" (1 John 3:1). May we learn to live more like it.

WHO *REALLY* BELIEVES?

The Bible says, "Repent, and let every one of you be baptized in the name of Jesus Christ for the remission of sins. . ." (Acts 2:38). Who ***really*** believes the Bible–the person who will be baptized for the remission of sins, or the person who refuses to do such?

The Bible says, "There is also an antitype which now saves us, namely baptism. . ." (1 Pet. 3:21). Who ***really*** believes the Bible–the person who acknowledges that baptism is involved in salvation, or the person who claims that baptism has nothing to do with salvation?

The Bible says, ". . . You have fallen from grace" (Gal. 5:4). Who ***really*** believes the Bible–the person who teaches that it is possible to fall from grace, or the person who says it is impossible for one to so sin as to fall from grace?

The Bible says, ". . . Speak the same thing" (1 Cor. 1:10). Who ***really*** believes the Bible–the person who says we can, and must, speak the same thing in religion, or the person who says "everyone has his own interpretation of the Bible," and thus it is impossible for people to be in agreement when it comes to what the Bible actually teaches?

The Bible says, "There is one body. . ." (Eph. 4:4) and this body is the church (Eph. 1:22-23). Who ***really*** believes the Bible–the person who teaches there is one church (one body), or the person who says "one church is as good as another?"

May each of us ask himself: Do I ***really*** believe the Bible?

THE TRUTH AND BEAUTY OF THE CHRISTIAN RELIGION

When in my early twenties, my paternal grandmother gave me a copy of a letter reported to have been written by the 19th century English novelist, Charles Dickens, to his youngest son when the boy left home to join his brother in Australia. In part, it read as follows:

> . . . Try to do to others as you would have them do to you, and do not be discouraged if they fail sometimes. It is much better for you that they should fail in obeying the greatest rule laid down by our Savior than that you should. I put a New Testament among your books for the very same reasons, and with the very same hopes, that made me write an easy account of it for you, when you were a little child. Because it is the best book that ever was, or will be, known in the world; and because it teaches you the best lessons by which any human creature, who tries to be truthful and faithful to duty, can possibly be guided. As your brothers have gone away, one by one, I have written to each such words as I am now writing to you, and have entreated them all to guide themselves by this Book, putting aside the interpretations and inventions of Man. You will therefore understand the better why I now most solemnly impress upon you the truth and beauty of the Christian Religion, as it came from Christ Himself and the impossibility of your going far wrong if you humbly but heartily respect it.

The above words are a reminder of one of the great needs in society, viz. the *recognition* of "the truth and beauty of the Christian Religion," and the *application* of the same. More personally, in one sense, it is the most pressing need you and I have in our lives. How are we doing? More of us likely need the humble attitude of another father who "said with tears, 'Lord, I believe, help my unbelief!'" (Mark 9:24).

WHAT IS THE CHURCH OF CHRIST?

Three days following His death on a Roman cross, Jesus of Nazareth presented Himself alive again. In fact, for more than a month, He established by many proofs that He had miraculously overcome death (Acts 1:3), appearing to several persons and to more than five hundred on one occasion (1 Cor. 15:6). At the end of forty days He ascended into Heaven before the eyes of eleven men who were to become great preachers in His church (Acts 1:9-11). Ten days following Jesus' ascension into Heaven, these men were gathered in the city of Jerusalem. It was the day known as the Jewish feast of Pentecost (Acts 2:1). There were thousands gathered in Jerusalem from every nation (Acts 2:5). As the apostles of the Christ were gathered together, a miracle occurred which enabled the apostles, though they were all Galileans (Acts 1:11; 2:7), to speak the foreign languages of the thousands who were gathered there in Jerusalem on that day. The apostles preached the death, burial, resurrection, ascension, and exaltation of Jesus (Acts 2:22-36). On that very day, three thousand were convinced of the truth concerning the identity of Jesus Christ, and they were baptized in His name for the forgiveness of their sins (Acts 2:37-39, 41).

It was on this historic day that the church of Christ had its beginning (Acts 11:15). Since then, the Lord has been adding to His church those who believe, repent, confess Him, and are baptized (immersed) for the forgiveness of sins (Acts 2:47). Those three thousand were added on the day of Pentecost, not to a denomination, but to the church of Christ, which is not a denomination. Denominations divide people (cf. 1 Cor. 1:10-13). We invite you to simply become a member of the church of Christ by doing what these did two thousand years ago.

Works Cited in Appendix:

Bales, James D. *Saul From Persecutor To Persecuted.* Shreveport: Lambert, 1975.

Bernard, J. H. *A Critical and Exegetical Commentary on The Gospel According To St. John.* 1928. Edinburgh: T&T Clark, 1958.

- - -. *The Expositors Greek Testament the Second Epistle to the Corinthians.* Vol. 3. London: Hodder and Stoughton, 1903. 5 vols.

Boettner, Loraine. *Immortality.* 1956. Philadelphia: The Presbyterian and Reformed Publishing Co., 1979.

Campbell, Alexander. "Religious Controversy". *The Millennial Harbinger.* 1830. Volume I. Joplin: College Press, n.d.

Centerville Messenger. Vol. 23, No. 11. Centerville: Centerville Church of Christ, 2002.

Duncan, Henry. *Sacred Philosophy of the Seasons Illustrating the Perfections of God in the Phenomena of the Year; Autumn.* New York: Robert Carter & Brothers, 1856.

- - -. *Sacred Philosophy of the Seasons Illustrating the Perfections of God in the Phenomena of the Year; Spring.* New York: Robert Carter & Brothers, 1856.

Fant, David J. *The Bible in New York.* New York: New York Bible Society, 1948.

Green, Michael. *Man Alive!.* 1946. Chicago: Inter-Varsity, 1968.

Haley, John W. *An Examination of the Alleged Discrepancies of the Bible.* Nashville: Gospel Advocate, 1967.

Hardeman, N. B. *Hardeman's Tabernacle Sermons.* Vol. 2. Nashville: Gospel Advocate, 1971. 5 vols.

Havner, Vance. *Seasonings.* Old Tappan: Fleming H. Revell Co., 1970.

Haygood, Atticus G. *The Man of Galilee*. 1889. Marion: Cogdill Foundation Publications,1963.

Hendricksen, William. *The Bible on the Life Hereafter*. 1959. Grand Rapids: Baker, 1975.

Henley, Ralph T. "B. C. Goodpasture's Last Reading Material." *The Gospel Advocate.* 119 (1977) : 585.

Lee, Robert G. *Grapes from Gospel Vines.* Nashville: Broadman, 1976.

- - -. *The Top Ten of Robert G. Lee*. 1971. Grand Rapids: Baker, 1976.

Lockyer, Herbert. *Last Words of Saints and Sinners.* 1969. Grand Rapids: Kregel, 1975.

Mitchell, Graham, *The Young Man's Guide Against Infidelity*. Edinburgh: William Whyte &Co., 1848.

Morris, A. J. *The Bible: What Is It?*. London: John F. Shaw & Co., n.d.

Osbeck, Kenneth W. *101 Hymn Stories*. Grand Rapids: Kregel, 1982.

Pfeiffer, Charles F. *The Human Side of the Saints*. Grand Rapids: Baker, 1976.

Plumer, Wm. S. *The Bible True, And Infidelity Wicked*. New York: The American Tract Society, n. d.

Pusey, E. B. *The Minor Prophets*. New York: Funk and Wagnalls, 1885.

Renan, Ernest. *The Life of Jesus*. 1863. Buffalo: Prometheus Books, 1991.

Richardson, Robert. *Memoirs of Alexander Campbell.* Philadelphia: J.B. Lippincott, 1870.

Robertson, Archibald Thomas. *Word Pictures in The New Testament.* Vol. 2. Grand Rapids: Baker, 1930. 6 vols.

Russell, Howard H. *A Lawyer's Examination of the Bible*. Chicago: Fleming H. Revell Company, 1893.

Sweeney, Z.T. *New Testament Christianity.* Vol. 2. Columbus: New Testament Christianity Book Fund, Inc., 1926. 3 vols.

Sweeting, George. "Moody and Ingersoll." *Moody Monthly*. 97.2 (1996) : 100.

Torrey, R. A. *The Bible and Its Christ*. New York: Fleming H. Revell Company, 1904.

Turner, Rex A., Sr. *Daniel: A Prophet Of God.* Montgomery: Southern Christian University, 1993.

Warren, Thomas B. and Antony G. N. Flew. *The Warren-Flew Debate on the Existence of God.* Jonesboro: National Christian Press, 1977.

West, Gilbert. *Observations on the History and Evidences of the Resurrection of Jesus Christ*. London: Tully's Head in Pall-Mall, 1747.

SCRIPTURE INDEX